W9-BIT-131

"If you talk to a man
in a language
he understands,
that goes to his head.

If you talk to him
in *his* language,
that goes to his heart."

NELSON MANDELA

RAISE YOUR VOICE

A CAUSE MANIFESTO

Brian Sooy

RockBench | Nashville | 2014

Praise for *Raise Your Voice: a Cause Manifesto*

"Finally, a great marketing book for charitable organizations. Brian Sooy brings clarity and structure to the challenge of branding a cause."

Marty Neumeier, *The Brand Gap*

"With *Raise Your Voice*, Brian Sooy has given designers, writers, and other creative professionals a highly relevant manifesto for cause-based and purpose-driven marketing. His ideas have important implications for leveraging the power of design to move people—in the nonprofit sector, higher education, and any other category where decisions are made with a blend of heart and mind."

Bill Faust, Managing Partner, Ologie

"Now more than ever, effectiveness in the marketplace depends on our ability to rise above the noise and cut through the clutter. Brian Sooy provides a practical, design-driven approach for sharing your message with clarity and passion."

Todd Henry, *Die Empty: Unleash Your Best Work Every Day*

"*Raise Your Voice* is a must-read for any organization that wants to align their message with their mission. You will learn how to create a culture that reinforces your organization's reason for existence—the cause that drives all aspects of a nonprofit endeavor."

Shannon D. Smith, Executive Director,
Wyoming Humanities Council

"Whether you're passionate about making a difference in education, philanthropy, the arts, or the church, I strongly suggest you grab a highlighter and a cup of coffee, and read carefully through the hard-earned insights Brian shares. Trust me, you're going to want to keep *Raise Your Voice* close at hand as you set about to change the world."

Scott Humphreys, Writer/Editor, Research Planning
and Marketing Team at GoodSeed International

"Every church is passionate about clearly communicating their message and mission. *Raise Your Voice* gives ministry leaders all the tools to communicate effectively and be heard in a noisy world."

Chet Beetler, Pastor, Christ Church, Ohio

"Part of what brings a donor to a cause is the hope of being part of a greater good. With *Raise Your Voice*, Brian Sooy gives nonprofits a means to go beyond being the loudest voice in the room to crafting a clear, articulate message which allows donors to see themselves as part of the solution."

Julie Chase-Morefield, Executive Director,
Second Harvest Food Bank of North Central Ohio

RockBench Publishing Corp.

6101 Stillmeadow Dr., Nashville, TN 37211

rockbench.com

Printed in the United States of America

Published 2014 | First Printing

Published simultaneously in electronic format

Library of Congress Control Number: 2014931614

ISBN-13: 978-1-60544-029-3

Visit causemanifesto.org for resources, inspiration, and a
complimentary Cause Manifesto poster that you can download.

Connect with Aespire® and Brian Sooy:

aespire.com | @aespire | @briansooy

rockbench

P U B L I S H I N G

courageous thought leadership content

For Lisa, you inspire me.

Sola gratia, Solus Christos, Soli Deo gloria.

A Designer's (and Designed Thinking) Approach to Advancing Your Cause

This is not a how-to book.

It's not specifically a book about positioning, design, fundraising, marketing, or social media—although each of these topics are discussed, and an essential element of finding your voice and engaging your audience. There are an abundance of how-to resources available via the Internet, for free or for a small fee.

As you read, consider this book to be a series of conversations. It's my intention that they are thought-provoking conversations, to influence you to change the way you think, and perhaps motivate you to act in a different way.

Isn't that your goal? To change the way people think, and change their behavior, in response to your meaningful cause?

I've talked with nonprofit leaders, executive directors, marketing and communications officers, development directors, volunteers, and board members. We all share one thing in common: to make a meaningful and lasting difference in our communities and in the world. I'm confident that every reader will find insights that will help them advance their cause.

This is a book about communicating better: speaking with one voice on behalf of a meaningful cause. It's about finding clarity. It's about telling inspiring and informative stories about outcomes and impact that create credibility. This book will give you insight into how to connect your purpose and mission with people whose values you share, and to bring meaning to their lives as they become ambassadors for your cause. It's about earning trust, and building relationships.

It's a book that will help you find your voice.

The heart may inspire you to start a journey, and your mind will guide you along the path. You must begin your journey with the end in mind. Every step along the way, every decision made, must be on the path between where you start and the goal you seek to accomplish at the end of your journey.

Mission-driven design will guide you to your goal, as a catalyst for cause communications that empowers you to connect with your audience. It will help you assess your progress and keep your eye focused on the destination. It is a compass to keep you on the path of communicating with clarity.

Design thinking is a guide to help you be aware of the context, consistency, and continuity of your marketing and communications, in light of the outcomes of your mission.

The journey is long; fulfilling your purpose and achieving your mission is the destination. Be certain you know where you are going so you can recognize it when you arrive.

Seeking Clarity

Every day, no matter where you are in the world, meaningful causes are trying harder than ever to get noticed, to rise above the noise, inspire change, motivate action, and speak with one voice.

The organizations that are the voice of these causes are looking to attract and acquire new donors and engage their communities. They are trying to raise awareness about who they are, what they do, and why they matter.

They are simply trying to communicate better.

Each one is trying to differentiate itself from other similar organizations, and show the difference that they are making. Churches, charities, schools, philanthropies, colleges, universities, and a host of other tax-exempt entities are trying to raise awareness about the cause they represent, and to raise funds to support their mission and programs.

No two organizations are alike, even if their mission and cause are closely related. Each will have a distinct purpose, each is defined by unique values and character, and all operate with a unique culture. Their cause and purpose are expressed through the design, marketing, and media choices they make. Their voice and language—the tone and personality—is heard through their words and made visible through their actions.

If this sounds distinctly human, it is. A nonprofit should not be perceived as a soulless corporation, but as a group of individuals who want to make a difference, to change the world, and to have an impact in the lives of people for generations to come.

Many nonprofits look to adapt the methods and means of marketing that are used to sell products and services. While there are excellent lessons to be learned from marketing best practices, have you ever considered that there might be a more insightful way to think about nonprofit communication?

YOU ARE WHAT THEY THINK YOU ARE

How your cause is perceived is directly related to how well the organization is perceived. Communication occurs in every way imaginable, and every touch point of communication creates a new (or reinforces an existing) perception.

Personally, we communicate through body language, facial expression, tone of voice, the way we dress, and how we act. Our thoughts, beliefs, and values are revealed by what we say and how we say it. What we feel in our heart—passion, compassion, empathy—contributes to the tone of how we communicate.

Your organization communicates with your audience through every verbal, visual, digital, printed, and experiential touch point, whether you intend to or not. Examples of touch points are your web site, printed materials, press releases, social networks, events, and conversations.

You may think your organization communicates well. You may think each design touch point is strategic, well executed, and compelling. Some may be informative, but not inspirational.

Have you asked and listened to what your audience has to say about how well you communicate? Have you asked your audience what you could do to communicate better?

Communication is directly related to design. Communication is the *what* (we are going to share); design is the *how* (we are going to share it). Together they create your organizational voice.

> Design choices must be purposeful and intentional, exist for the cause, be driven by the mission, and be guided by the purpose for which the organization exists.

Every touch point has a purpose. Every interaction your audience has with staff, leadership, events, or media has to be intentional—designed with the thought that it has the potential to create or steward a relationship.

Design creates opportunities. Touch points are opportunities to share a message, open hearts, open minds. Design cannot be left to chance.

Design choices must be purposeful and intentional, exist for the cause, be driven by the mission, and be guided by the purpose for which the organization exists.

Design contributes to culture, from the moment a new

staff member, donor, volunteer, or advocate reads, sees, hears, or interacts with your organization.

Culture creates ambassadors. Ambassadors have a connection to the organization, and a love of the cause. They are advocates. They will wear apparel emblazoned with your logo, with tag lines and phrases designed to inspire and motivate. They will speak out passionately and enthusiastically, sharing the words and messages that you have communicated so well to them.

Where there are many messages, design helps prioritize them, magnify them, and visualize them. Design turns information into inspiration, blends images and words into stories, and stories into shared experiences.

Perhaps you are a nonprofit leader or executive, a volunteer, or a director on a nonprofit board. Perhaps you're a donor to a cause you find meaningful. You're involved because you believe you can create change; because you felt you wanted to give back to the community; to make a difference. You believe you can contribute to the cultural or to the greater good. These are noble reasons.

From these perspectives—as a leader, volunteer, director, or donor—what principles of communication can convey trust, gratitude, courage, and help advance the cause?

How can you inspire your followers and give them a reason to believe in your cause?

COMMUNICATING WITH CLARITY

Every meaningful cause needs several components to move it forward: **Purpose** (why it exists), **Mission and Vision** (how and what you have set out to achieve), **Goals and Outcomes** (specific things you are going to accomplish), and **Strategy** (the tactics you will use to achieve your goals and outcomes).

There is a thread that weaves these components together, that aligns the internal voice with the external listeners. This thread has many strands, or principles, that when woven together form a strong cord that bind the cause to its ambassadors, its stakeholders, and its advocates.

I discovered this thread after many conversations with nonprofit leaders who were searching for a way to articulate a clear and focused idea of the purpose, character, and culture of their organization. These leaders understand their organization's purpose, but struggle at times to fully connect that purpose with their audience. They understand what they are on a mission to do, but are challenged by how to effectively share how their cause is different and how their organization makes a difference.

What they are searching for is *clarity*.

Clarity is the clear and focused path for communication, the bridge between the cause and its followers. When an organization can find clarity, it finds its unique voice, confidently speaking and acting on behalf of the cause it represents.

Clarity can help transform the internal culture of an organization and energize the staff. Clarity can contribute to the difference in a nonprofit's performance as it finds a new voice and ways of expression on behalf of its cause. Clarity can guide an effective communication plan that stewards existing relationships and creates new relationships. Clarity can help build affinity, loyalty, and trust with followers.

What are *you* searching for?

Ambassadors, Advocates, and Your Biggest Fans

Several years ago, I was invited to join the board of directors of our regional food bank. At the first board meeting I attended, I didn't have a clear understanding of the cause or my role. I didn't fully understand the focus of, or the mission of the organization. I did not understand that my role was to be an *ambassador* for the organization and an *advocate* for the cause.

Yet over the last few years, I've learned an effective board is as enthusiastic about the cause, as it is about providing effective business leadership of the organization. A well-led board understands strategy, governance, and oversight. A forward-thinking board empowers the executive leadership with resources to effectively communicate its strategic objectives and outcomes.

What nonprofits need are fewer individuals who serve on multiple boards, and more individuals committed to serving effectively on one or two boards. Your participation on a board should not be based solely on your title, circles of influence or income, but also on your commitment to the cause.

While board members often serve enthusiastically, and provide excellent governance and oversight, the forward-thinking aspect of their role—empowering for effective communications—doesn't always happen.

FACE PAINT AND FANTASY LEAGUES

Imagine for a moment the particular nonprofit you have in mind is like a sports team: You want people on the team who desire—more than anything—for their team to win. Teams are made up of coaches and managers; cheerleaders; players and support staff; and, of course, the fans.

Like coaches and managers, the board and executive staff will work together to ensure the success of the team. They represent the team on the field, off the field, in the media, and at social and business events.

First and foremost, each member of the board of directors is an advocate for the cause and an ambassador of the organization. They must be fluent in the purpose, mission, and key talking points (the story); and be able to speak with one voice for the cause.

Engaged sports fans refer to the team as "my team." They wear face paint; they sport the team colors; fans attend every game (some will travel hundreds of miles to attend games); they give of their time ("volunteering" time for game attendance or viewing); they buy tickets and merchandise (in effect, they donate); and they spend time, even at work (but not you of course), playing fantasy league games.

These are more than fans—they are believers. Believers don't just participate in team culture, they contribute sacrificially to the culture. The team is a priority in many aspects of their lives.

What would it take to inspire your board to become the sacrificial ambassadors of your nonprofit culture? And what would it take to create a legion of fans that support not just the organization, but also the cause—fervently and sacrificially?

This can (and does) occur when there is clarity in a nonprofit's communications, when everyone involved—from the board to staff to volunteers—is clear about the strategic plan, its objectives, and how they are going to be achieved. It's especially critical for organizations that are run by the board (those without paid staff), who need a guiding plan to keep them on track while they are busy fulfilling the nonprofit's mission. It's even more important for the board that is charged with governance and oversight. It is a powerful combination when the members of the board and the executive staff have the same goals, and are in agreement with regard to design and communication strategy.

> These are more than fans—they are believers. Believers don't just participate in team culture, they contribute sacrificially to the culture. The team is a priority in many aspects of their lives.

Communicating well assures that the board, the staff, and the external stakeholders know what the mission is, how it's going to be achieved, and what it will be like when it becomes reality.

But how do you find clarity?

BEGINNING WITH THE END IN MIND

I have had the privilege of working with a young couple who were in the process of forming a philanthropic foundation. Over coffee, the husband—who had been a colleague for many years—explained why he and his wife had decided to found a new nonprofit.

The founders had made good progress: they had a name for their foundation and a board of directors, and were awaiting the approval of their 501(c)3 application. In the meantime, they were holding fundraisers to continue to do the good work they want to accomplish.

Working with their board, the couple had created a mission statement and captured a few statistics that supported the mission. Now they were looking for direction. They had a great idea and put their plans into motion, but—by their own admission—they were still lacking something. When I asked what it was that they were looking for, the husband's response was "We need *clarity*."

Even at this early stage in their process, the founders recognized that although the idea and organization were in place, it still needed focus. From their perspective, they had a distinct mission; in their minds, clarity would provide validation.

What they were doing made perfect sense to them; the next step was to begin to think about how they would communicate their cause and mission to the world. Our first step would be to articulate their purpose, which would make certain that they stayed focused and able to share their mission clearly with their audiences.

I challenged the couple to consider what made their foundation unique; what qualities made it different from others that may be similar. Beyond that, what *difference* would it make in the lives of those whom it benefited?

The focus of the mission in many respects was about doing: "We are this and we will do this and this." To get them to think beyond what they would *do*, I asked them "What is the cause that the foundation stands for, and why does this foundation matter?"

What difference will your cause make in the lives of those you touch?

> The essence of clarity is to be clear—driven by purpose, focused on mission, and articulate in communication.

The outcome of clarity is focused communication. Clarity can give you the ability to gain perspective. Clarity creates the stage to help articulate that perspective for those who are inside the organization, and to understand how the cause is perceived by those "outside the bottle."

Every organization has stories to tell (not just *a* story). What brings continuity to the stories is the narrative—one voice that weaves the stories together in order to create continuity and cohesiveness.

Each organization's voice is unique—as when you answer your phone and recognize the caller without having to ask whom it is. Yet during that call, the caller is not telling you the same story (then again, maybe they are, and you just have to listen to it again). They're sharing a new story or simply news, or inviting you somewhere, or perhaps just wanted to hear your voice.

Clarity creates the context for a nonprofit to become the one voice of a cause, so that it is able to share many stories. The nonprofit, through that voice, creates credibility by sharing the cause from the heart (its values and character), and validates it through facts that speak to the mind.

Clarity speaks to the mind to *inform* (reason) and appeals to the heart to *inspire* (emotions). When you (or an organization or cause) are perceived as credible, then you are trusted. When you are trusted, your audience is more likely to believe you, and trust their interactions with you.

> **Clarity speaks to the mind to *inform* (reason) and appeals to the heart to *inspire* (emotions).**

It seems like a simple approach to communications, and perhaps it is. Not everybody understands the complexities and practices of marketing; not every nonprofit professional has communication experience. But everybody can understand the dynamics of relationships and conversations.

It's possible that in your organization, design and communications are an afterthought, or a low priority. Perhaps in your organization, marketing communications are seen as a luxury, and not as a critical component to advancing the cause or achieving the mission.

You'll find that the most effective nonprofits are those in which the board and staff have a clear understanding of the mission and believe that communication is critical to advancing the cause and achieving the mission.

Now, let's continue the story of this new foundation.

Inspiration Starts at the Top

I noted that the couple made some notes at this point in our conversation. Clearly this idea of clarity struck a chord.

Ultimately, any nonprofit—whether it's a foundation, a church, a college, or a charity—has two goals: create sustainable impact through their mission; and raise awareness, funds, and resources to advance their mission. The audience (volunteers, advocates, donors, and future board members) wants assurance that the organization is credible, and wants to believe the cause is worth investing in. Supporters want to know the organization is truthful, trustworthy, transparent, and accountable. When an organization demonstrates credibility (and is not just *perceived* as credible), trust follows.

Clarity is critical because every nonprofit advocates for something much bigger: a greater purpose than its own existence, or an issue or cause that has the potential to affect change and have an impact on many individuals.

In the future, the story of why this particular foundation was formed will be a memory—one couple's unique experience and story—but the cause it represents is much more profound and compelling, and will be inspirational as long as the issue exists.

Future donors, volunteers, and advocates may not connect with or be connected with the *memory* of the founders (the couple who started the foundation), but they may connect with the *experience* of the founders and the cause. They may be inspired by the story of why the foundation was started, but never know the founders.

Future donors, volunteers, and followers will want to support the cause in order to bring change to the circumstances and situation that created this issue.

As with any nonprofit, the founder's story may be a memory, but the purpose for which the foundation was formed will continue until the issue is solved.

KEY INSIGHT

Imagine filling in this sentence on behalf of your organization: "We are an organization that speaks on behalf of **(the cause)**. The reason we exist is to serve this **(higher purpose)**. We will make a difference through **(our mission)**. The outcome will be **(our vision)**."

Meaningful causes are led by board members and leaders who share a passion for change, and who unite with common purpose to solve an issue. These leaders make decisions that empower the organization to effectively communicate with clarity to outcomes, manage sustainable support for the cause, and create an identity that becomes the personal and familiar voice of the cause.

The mission will describe how the organization will work to address the issue of the cause. The cause is the greater issue that the organization advocates for. It is in the combination of cause and mission that the organization will find purpose.

WHERE DOES THE CONVERSATION BEGIN?

At this point, I had to ask the founders: "Is the board inspired?"

I wanted to know *who* is on the board, and *why* they wanted to be on the board (not who they wanted on the board, or the reason they wanted them on the board).

If the board is not informed or inspired, critical motivation for the success of the organization may be missing. The board may not understand the true nature of the cause, or how this particular organization is qualified to be its voice and achieve its mission. If they don't understand, they won't be inspired or motivated to act.

A working board (one in which each individual is completely engaged, advocating for the cause, and speaking as an ambassador) is one that will give proper oversight and governance. This kind of board will properly fund engagement and outreach, and empower the president or executive director to guide effective communications (through funding, resources, and as a partner in the cause).

The board must be ambassadors for the organization, and fully able to speak as an advocate for the cause. The board also has to commit to funding and empowering the organization to be the voice of the cause. The board has to be committed.

In this instance, the members of the board were inspired by the experience of the young couple, and informed enough to address the cause and its significance. One individual was a physician; two were attorneys. It was not a large board, but their reasons for participating on the board were compelling.

This particular foundation was created in honor of the memory of the couple's eight year-old son, who lost his fight with cancer in the previous year. Their experience as parents, and the challenges they faced in visits to the health care facility where their son was treated—even their *choice* of health care provider—compelled them to start a foundation that could provide assistance for families in similar situations, and influence change in how health care systems care for children with cancer.

The young physician serving on their board had been on the team that had cared for their son while he was undergoing cancer treatments. He and the couple's son had formed a close, personal bond during the treatment process.

Through tears, the couple explained that the physician still missed their son, and was very moved by their commitment to honoring and celebrating their son's life in this way. He wanted to see them succeed in helping other parents maintain a sense of family during the difficulties of cancer treatment.

The attorney who was on the board had approached the parents about helping, and had significant experience in working with donors and family foundations.

One of the most memorable points in our conversation

was when the founders shared how difficult it had become for other families to afford the expense of parking at the urban hospital they had chosen for the care of their son. The hospital's children's services coordinator shared with them that the president of the health care institution had decided that there would be no more parking passes, even for families with children. They wondered how other families who may not be as fortunate as they were could afford to park; cancer knew no socio-economic boundaries.

To this challenge, one of the board members remarked: *"We'll raise enough money to buy a parking garage."*

It was clear to this small group of individuals the cause was bigger than the memory of the couple's son. It was about families who have to maintain a sense of normalcy during the difficult times of choosing a cancer treatment path; of choosing a health care facility; and of trips to health care systems geared toward adult treatment and not toward families and the care of children. It was about children, and the hope that every parent has for their child's future.

It only takes a small spark to start a fire. It only takes a few passionate individuals to start a movement.

MEANING THROUGH CLARITY

At times, clarity is arrived at through tears. The tears wash away the residue of distraction and allow the eyes to focus on the true cause, the purpose for which an organization exists, and the reasons why it matters.

Arriving at clarity shouldn't require tears. There are timeless communication principles that enable nonprofit organizations to see the path that is most appropriate for them to follow. While on that path, your organization must communicate how it is best suited to address its cause and achieve its mission.

Inspiration starts with the board. It doesn't take much for the inspiration to spread when founders and executive directors are confident that the board is committed to the cause.

MISSION-DRIVEN DESIGN THINKING

The purpose of this conversation is to help board members, executive directors, and nonprofit professionals understand what is required to empower the organization to communicate with clarity. It is a perspective that will help your audience clearly understand your purpose and how it will have a meaningful and lasting impact.

It's *beyond branding* and *more than storytelling*.

Mission-driven design is a path to informing donors, advocates, and participants, by inspiring them to action and engaging them as ambassadors for your nonprofit. It's about making conscious decisions about how and what to communicate with your audience, because you understand what motivates them to support your cause, based on research and insight. Mission-driven design is about design choices and media touch points that deliver your message to ears that are eager to hear it. Perhaps your organization will grow as it understands its purpose, character, and culture in a whole new way.

It's an opportunity to raise your voice and be heard in a noisy culture.

Knowing When to Raise Your Voice

USING MEANINGFUL WORDS

"Mom! Dad! She said the 'S' word!"

That would be the tattle-tale voice of my son, when he and his sister were disagreeing. When my children were younger, my wife and I had a rule of not using the "S" word in our home. Perhaps you have a similar rule, so your children learn the importance, value, and weight of language. In our home, the "S" word was *stupid*. (What were *you* thinking it was?) We did not want our children to use negative words as part of their vocabulary, and constantly taught them how words are meaningful.

"PLEASE USE YOUR INSIDE VOICE!"

Likewise, we value tone of voice. There's a time to shout, a time to raise your voice, and a time to whisper. We taught our children how to have adult conversations, how to communicate respectfully and with conviction. Knowing when and how to speak adds urgency and meaning to the words that are spoken.

Tone of voice is evident in any touch point your audience has with your organization—anything your audience reads, sees, hears, or experiences. Your organization gives voice to the cause. In an organization's eagerness to "brand," its voice is often overlooked.

A DIFFERENT PERSPECTIVE

Branding has become less meaningful as the "B" word is used as a catchall for many aspects of visual communications. People talk of their brand, of re-branding, of creating a brand. For the most part, these individuals are speaking of identity and logos, without a clear understanding of the discipline of branding.

Instead of branding, the focus should be on identity and personality. A nonprofit should be more concerned about its positioning—how it wants to be perceived by its audience and supporters. It must be aware of what truly makes it different—and the difference it is in a position to make.

Let's agree at this point to avoid the "B" word, and instead talk about visual language and verbal language; messages and stories; tone of voice and audience perception; and of touch points and design language. Let's talk about how these elements help build relationships.

From this point on, our conversation will be guided by *mission-driven design, identity,* and *personality.* Design is a visual language. Messages are conveyed through visual and verbal language. Tone of voice imparts meaning. The conversation and interactions with your audience need to be very human-centered (a key principle of design thinking).

But first, let's explore a different perspective.

CONTROLLING THE UNCONTROLLABLE

An organization cannot always control how it is perceived, but it can control its voice. According to Marty Neumeier, "A brand is a person's gut feeling about a product, service, or organization. The brand isn't what you say it is. It's what they say it is."

Consider this perspective: "*Your cause is worthy, and becomes meaningful when your audience says it is.*"

In your mind, you know your cause is worthy, and it's important to you. It's meaningful to you, and becomes meaningful to your audience as they begin to form a relationship with your organization.

But there are two parts to the equation:

An organization's beliefs and practices
+ What the audience perceives, hears, and experiences
_____

= The perception of a meaningful cause

At any given time, what your organization is thinking, saying, and doing may not match what your audience perceives, hears, and sees. That is why communicating with clarity is so critical.

Over time, as your organization speaks on behalf of the cause, the audience hears its voice. It is over time that your organization is perceived as the voice of the cause, because of what the audience hears and sees.

The cause becomes more meaningful to those who choose to follow, as what is said and heard aligns with what motivates the audience to believe. The cause becomes more meaningful to society when the audience is engaged. Through their support, the organization has resources to make its impact even greater.

HUNGER IS NOT A BRAND

You're thinking:
- "But we have this great brand."
- "But the board recommended that we re-brand."
- "But we just finished a branding campaign."

But, but, but. What you're thinking about is your organization.

The cause of ending hunger is not a brand. Neither are the causes of education, economic development, clean water, AIDS prevention and cure, cancer awareness, human trafficking, faith, the arts, health, food and nutrition, social issues, sustainability, youth development, or social action.

A cause is not a brand.

Consider the circumstances of people facing cancer or advocating for cancer research, cure, and awareness: is it appropriate to consider their circumstance as a brand, or as a meaningful cause?

To view it as a brand means that we need to position it, market it, and promote it. Viewing your cause as a brand demeans it. It's devoid of meaning, and neither informs nor inspires.

- To a woman going through the journey of healing, cancer is not a brand.

- To a child who relies on a backpack of donated food so that she can have breakfast on Saturday, hunger is not a brand.
- To the victims of human trafficking, their circumstance is not a brand.
- To the citizens of any region of the world, economic development is not a brand.
- *The cause is not a brand.*

Your organization is not a brand. It is the *voice* of your cause.

Your organization is a group of committed volunteers, professionals, and ambassadors who want to achieve significant impact. Your organization is an advocate that needs to rise above the noise, motivate action, and speak with one voice. Your followers and supporters want to follow a higher purpose and be inspired.

> **Your cause is not a brand.**

A meaningful cause must follow principles of communication that flow from a place of higher purpose. A cause has no mission statement or vision statement; no board, no trustees, no staff. A cause has no logo, social media accounts, or marketing budget.

Your cause is bigger than a brand can ever be. In order to rise above the noise, your organization will have to find its voice in order to get noticed, inspire change, motivate your followers to action, and achieve greater impact.

IT'S TIME TO RAISE YOUR VOICE

Your organization can listen, and it can speak to the values it wants to share with its followers. It can listen and hear what values its followers are looking for. It is in conversation about the cause where supporters realize that their values align with the cause, where trust and loyalty are formed and long-lasting relationships are built.

Verbal messages are shared through visual language, with a unique tone of voice.

Any organization that acts and speaks on behalf of a worthy cause, becomes the voice of that cause. Through mission-driven design and clarity of communication, the audience begins to associate the organization as the voice for the cause, and experience how it communicates on its behalf. Through the audience's engagement with the organization, the cause becomes meaningful. The audience experiences the cause through your organization's purpose, its character, and its culture. It learns about the cause through the organization's voice and visual language.

This is how perception is formed. Cause communication flows from principles of higher purpose. These communication principles are a deep foundation upon which a successful organization's voice is formed.

Repeating the Same Conversations

WHY IS THERE CONFUSION?

In offices and boardrooms around the world, the same conversations are taking place every day. Most of the time, the conversations are about *perceived* communications problems, instead of *defining what the problem actually is.*

Many organizations want to raise their voice before they understand how to communicate with their audience. Few succeed. Many struggle.

How would *you* respond to these statements?

- "We need clarity."
- "We think we need your help with branding."
- "We need a communications road map."
- "We've got this really great opportunity to…"
- "I wish my board would let me move forward without reviewing everything I do."

- "We've always done it this way. It just isn't working as well as before."
- "The board thinks we need to re-brand."
- "We have great programs but our target audience doesn't know they exist."
- "We need to tell our story."
- "We need a social media presence."
- "We need to market to donors."

These are excellent conversation starters. *Here's how I would respond:*

- "We need clarity." *If so, are you willing to focus on your mission, and eliminate things that are distractions from your real purpose?*
- "We think we need your help with branding." *Let's do some research and find out what other people think about you. Then we'll find your voice.*
- "We need a communications road map." *Let's not be too eager to create a map before we know what the destination is.*
- "We've got this really great opportunity to…" *How does that fit into your mission and purpose? Are you willing to take the tough step of saying no and eliminating potential opportunities?*
- "I wish my board would let me move forward without reviewing everything I do." *Sounds like the board never completed the strategic plan. The board doesn't know where the organization is headed.*
- "We've always done it this way. It just isn't working as well as before." *That's called a sacred cow. Sacred cows make great steak dinners. Which of yours would you like to dig into first?*

- "The board thinks we need to re-brand." *Branding is for products and corporations. Your cause is not a brand. We think you need to define your cause, and articulate your purpose, character, and culture. Then you'll be closer to finding your voice.*
- "We have great programs but our audience doesn't seem to know they exist." *Either you are telling the wrong story or talking to the wrong audience. Or both.*
- "We need to tell our story." *We think you need to find your voice before you tell your stories.*
- "We need a social media presence to solve this problem." *Social media will not solve all your problems. Tell me about the relationships you're building, and how you're building them.*
- "We need to market to donors." *All communications are donor communications. You started marketing to them a long time ago.*
- "I want to articulate our values, but I am having a hard time doing so, even though they are in my head." *Make a list to get them out of your head and on paper. Then we can explore if those values are reflected in your culture.*

Not every organization needs clarity to the same extent, but there will be at least one place where the communications gap can be bridged though a holistic approach and a series of choices designed to close that gap.

WE JUST NEED TO DO MORE MARKETING

The singular focus of the marketing committee of a nonprofit board is often just that: *marketing.*

The board and the staff need to work together to become better *communicators.* The board can't place the outreach burden entirely on the leadership or attempt to create marketing or communication strategy without the staff's participation. Likewise, the leadership must encourage the board to provide the resources they require, including professional communications expertise. (The board may need to understand their role more clearly, and take their responsibilities more seriously for this to happen).

For a marketing committee traveling along a tactical path (doing before planning), it's easy to miss the full continuum of engagement, and look for easy tactical solutions without analyzing and defining the real communication problems.

The questions asked are often the wrong questions:

- How do we reach more donors? I heard that another nonprofit did this kind of fundraiser. Maybe we should try the same thing.
- Everybody is talking about social media. We need a social media presence.
- We need a new web site. Let's create an RFP, based on what we think we need. Does anybody know a web designer?

From experience, you and I know the former set of questions will create a lively discussion around each topic, as opinions are shared and tactical solutions are thrown out. A subcommittee will be formed. Action will precede strategy; doing will precede thinking.

Instead, the marketing committee should define the problem first, before attempting to seek a solution. The definitions and questions to ask might look more like this:

- Revenue from groups x and y are steady, but revenue from group z is much lower. In our market, with the type of donors we already reach, what new groups of potential donors should we seek? What are possible solutions for reaching those particular groups?

- The staff is limited to outreach on one social media platform. Should we even be on social media? Which one should we choose? How should we manage it so we can measure our return on engagement and influence?
- Let's hire an expert to diagnose our web site, our needs, and our audience. Our web site does not allow for online donations, and we have to pay an outside firm to manage it. What is the best content management solution based on our audience's needs, and our staff's capabilities? How will our audience be using the web site? How will our staff be using the web site? How could we use the web site more effectively to achieve our mission and serve our stakeholders?

Better yet, what if you disbanded the marketing committee and instead formed a communication committee? If that sounds far-fetched, read on.

The mission-driven design perspective requires a strategy of **Attracting**, **Informing**, **Inspiring**, and **Engaging** the audience. How else will you create a culture of stewardship for ambassadors, volunteers, advocates, and stakeholders that your nonprofit needs to help advance the cause?

IMAGINE A BETTER WAY TO COMMUNICATE

Imagine that your goal is more than marketing. Instead, imagine that your goal is to *build relationships*, through engagement, to arrive at stewardship.

KEY INSIGHTS (MORE AT CAUSEMANIFESTO.ORG)

> **Giving USA research** (givingusareports.org) highlights trends in giving and philanthropy, and is an excellent resource for correlating trends in your revenue analysis.
> **Hootsuite.com** is an excellent choice for social media management for nonprofits.
> **Twitonomy.com** can help you analyze the social media data.
> **Joomla!** is an open source content management system that is powerful enough for even the largest nonprofit or university.

Marketing is too often a one-way, short-term, transactional exercise. Relationships are built through conversations and interactions to engage your audience. Marketing may tend to drive one time interaction; relationship building encourages long-term engagement and stewardship. Marketing can be superficial; engaging people over the long-term helps to develop deep and meaningful relationships.

The goal is not marketing; the goal is *communication* leading to stewardship. Your communications need to be redefined and evaluated with this goal in mind. This is where the board and leadership begins to understand that in order to build affinity for the cause and loyalty for the organization, each and every touch point along the continuum is specific to and has a purpose for the intended audience. It's not a short-term process.

We can map engagement to a continuum, where audience and messaging are matched to the medium. (This is sometimes referred to as a Media Matrix or Media Box Model.)

When you view engagement as a continuum, you will find that marketing will need to *decrease* while relationship building will *increase*. Marketing will be seen as a tactical, short-term approach to promoting events and attracting new supporters, and that communication will support long-term relationship building. It will be the understanding of each board member that their role is to serve as an ambassador for the organization and an advocate for the cause. Through their leadership and management, the board will empower and equip the staff with the resources and funding necessary to advance the cause through design and a long-term, comprehensive communication strategy.

That may mean that the board will have to get more engaged with fundraising, because for many boards, marketing is the first expense to get cut, and the last to get reinstated.

It's a crucial shift in thinking for those board members who are in corporate positions, especially if they are marketing or communications professionals. Instead of talking the language of sales, marketing, and value propositions, the language in the nonprofit space is of outreach, engagement, relationships, and impact.

AN ALTERNATIVE PERSPECTIVE

Very few corporations or small businesses invest less than 1% of their budget in marketing and communication planning. Marketing and public relations investments are measured against sales revenue and company growth.

It's common in the nonprofit sector for the opposite to occur. According to survey results reported in *The Communications Toolkit*, 60% of nonprofits spend less than 1% of their budget on design and communication. Yet the board expects disproportionate returns on such a small investment.

Funders and nonprofit boards often share the perspective that design and communication are overhead expenses, and not program-related investments.

Nonprofits, fearful of rejection during the grant seeking process, are hesitant to include design and communication planning as part of their funding requests. Donors expect that their gifts will go to program support, and have not been educated to expect that design and communication are part of the program delivery.

The engagement continuum is made up of communications components (or touch points, the points where your communications touch your audience), donor engagement, and donor management. Marketing is just one of many components that begins with the organization's strategic plan (and the strategies and tactics associated with the goals).

Additional components include board outreach and advocacy, a strategic communication plan, mission-driven design, donor relations, fundraising, and other advancement objectives.

Engagement begins with understanding the cause, the organization the board represents, the culture of the organization, and the complexity of the cause or issue.

It's imperative that board members believe in the cause and the organization that they represent. It's critical for everyone to be able to articulate key elements of the organization's mission and reasons the organization is well positioned to address the cause.

Yet there are some funders, donors, and enlightened boards whose thinking has ascended, and who recognize that better design and communication choices lead to more sustainable nonprofits. They see the big picture, and are making funding, design, and communication choices to support the mission.

Will you be one of them?

RAISE YOUR VOICE

You Are Here: the Cause Quadrant

Think of all of the causes with which you are familiar (and with which your organization competes for funding and resources). In the broadest sense, causes fall into two categories: those in which your audiences are interested emotionally (what inspires us with compassion, what appeals to our hearts) or rationally (what informs us, speaking to our minds).

There are many reasons that motivate your audience's interest in your cause; it's rarely one extreme or the other, with many personal nuances in between. We're informed by what speaks to our minds and thoughts; we're inspired by what appeals to our hearts.

AN ALTERNATIVE MODEL FOR SELF-EVALUATION

The path to clarity in your communication starts with a general understanding of where the cause and the organization fit into the context of other tax-exempt entities.

The *National Taxonomy of Exempt Entities* (NTEE) Classification System (http://ow.ly/qI5Vo) classifies non-profit organizations based on the organizations' primary functions, and was developed by the National Center for Charitable Statistics. Organizations such as GuideStar and the Foundation Center use these codes as part of their classification criteria for evaluation, grants, and grant seekers. Coincidentally, the categories in the quadrant are similar to those reflected in Giving USA studies.

This taxonomy can also be used to position and gain perspective of your organization within the context of other meaningful causes and supporter motivations. It can be a useful reference point for evaluating the mix of inspirational and informative messaging in your design and communication planning.

THE RATIONALE

Researchers and fundraisers continually conduct studies and research donor motivations, in an attempt to quantify what motivates and influences individuals to support a particular cause.

My experience has shown that the NTEE classification can be segmented into a quadrant, with some general motivations as its axis. This is not an attempt to quantify motivations, but to help a nonprofit organization identify what mix of messaging may be appropriate for their cause, in the context of peers and competing organizations. In general, people support causes, and not institutions. Knowing what your perspective should be, competitively and experientially, is valuable. Your design choices and marketing communication will be more powerful if you understand what your perspective is, and your point of view when you speak.

Practically speaking, you will need to position your organization as the voice of the cause, within a crowded and noisy marketplace. You will need to demonstrate content expertise of the cause, and support it with communications about the organization.

NO MOTIVATIONS		
Human Services Health	Greater Good People	Public/Society Benefit Foundations Education
Emotional Appeal		Rational Appeal
Animals Environment Religion	Issues/Activities Cultural Good	Arts, Culture & Humanities International

The top half of the quadrant includes entities that impact people directly: health, human services, public/society benefit, foundations, and education. This is considered the greater good segment of entities.

The lower half of the quadrant includes entities that influence culture and special interests. These include animals; environment; religion; international; and arts, culture and humanities. This is considered the cultural good segment of entities.

Horizontally, those that fall on the left appeal primarily to our hearts, and those that fall on the right speak primarily to our minds. I've already stated that the appeal is not one extreme or the other; there are many nuances in between. We're informed by what speaks to our minds and thoughts; we're inspired by what appeals to our hearts.

WHERE DO YOU FIT IN?

Think about which one of the four quadrants into which your cause may fall. Does it work with basic human services? Human services falls into the top half of the quadrant. This cause may interest to those who are motivated to support this type of cause because it appeals to their heart.

Is yours an arts organization? Then perhaps your followers are passionate about supporting the arts. Beauty and the arts stir our hearts. If the cause speaks primarily to the mind, it falls into the rational-cultural good portion of the grid, because it does not meet a basic human need.

Is your cause affiliated with an association? It is most likely an organization supported out of interest for the group or field it represents; a rational-cultural good choice. Supporters are influenced by the opportunity to learn and associate with individuals who share their common interest.

Your personal experience may lead you to support the cause of cancer cure or research, which could fall into either the emotional or rational side of the quadrant.

As a last example, is it an animal related cause? If so, it may be an emotional-cultural good choice for individuals to support.

Once you've identified which quadrant into which your cause potentially falls, next consider what may generally motivate and influence your donors and supporters:

Factors that motivate and influence individuals to support and donate to a cause have been widely researched both in the United States and the United Kingdom. In order to help understand how to explain your mission to your audience, consider what factors may potentially motivate your audience to volunteer and support your cause.

If one thing is more important than any other it's this: seek to know and understand your audience and community. Every constituent group—millennial, baby boomers, retirees, alumni—are motivated and influenced by different, and often generation-specific, factors. You can't assume that *your* generational perspective is the same as others.

After researching donor and volunteer motivations, some patterns did emerge with regard to reasons and values. Some causes appeal to the heart more than they speak to the mind. Others speak to the mind—to inform before they inspire—and appeal to personal factors.

Ask some of your current donors and volunteers why they do what they do on behalf of your cause. The answers will give you great insight into how you can communicate more effectively with them.

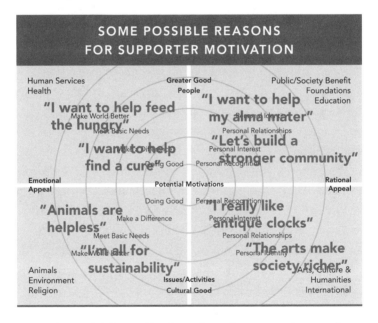

This model is qualitative—based on experience, observations, existing and new donor research, and observation. Consider it a starting point for a fresh perspective on how your cause may appeal to your audience, informing the choices you make for design and communication planning.

WHAT'S THE POINT?

The quadrant can help you to place your cause and organization into its context in the competitive landscape, with other similar or different organizations. A basic understanding of the emotional/rational balance of your messaging will help you to inspire *and* inform—creating a narrative and identifying stories that build credibility.

> Your audience is listening for a voice that speaks to their mind and appeals to their heart.

Lean too heavily on emotion, and you risk losing potential supporters who respond to messages that speak to their intellect. If you rely too much on information and knowledge-based messaging, your stories may appear boring to an individual who needs an emotional appeal to their heart.

What you want to find is the right balance of emotional and rational messaging that creates a voice of credibility. Understanding your communications context will help you to create a narrative that informs *and* inspires. The most powerful stories are those that combine three elements: pathos (emotion), logos (rationality), and ethos (credibility). Emotion and rationality, woven into the narrative, builds credibility for your organization and your cause. (See the Cause Manifesto principle, *Be Powerful*.)

The challenge is to stop thinking like a *brand* and *define your personality* in order to *create your identity* and *find your voice*. Remember, a cause is not a brand. Yours is a mission-driven organization, advocating on behalf of a meaningful cause, operating with character, values, and a culture that give your audience reason to believe in your cause and support your purpose. Your organization must become the voice for those who have no voice.

SPEAKING WITH ONE VOICE

A colleague asked: "Is it more important for people to believe in the cause or the individual?"

My response: "Every cause needs a voice, every organization needs a face."

We all know dynamic, inspirational figures that lead organizations we support or serve in. We follow pastors, executive directors, presidents, and other leaders who speak fluently and coherently on behalf of the cause for which they are advocates.

The nonprofit is the voice of the cause, because it can often have a bigger voice than an individual. At the same time, an individual can be the face of the organization. He or she will be the lead ambassador, and set the example for all others, from the board to the staff.

Both the cause and the organization are important. The organization will always speak on behalf of the cause; it's critical for your audience to understand the difference between the two, and how they work together.

Remember, your audience may at first perceive a difference between the cause and the organization, but over time will associate your organization with the cause.

In the same way, over time your audience may associate an individual with your organization. That individual becomes a familiar face for the cause.

For example: Hunger is a worldwide problem. Your local food bank will address the needs of those at risk for hunger in your community and region, and distribute food to the local food pantries. Food pantries will work to meet the need of distributing food to families in need. Other non-government and food relief organizations will address the issue of hunger in developing countries. Your audience knows the difference. If they want to support hunger relief, they will choose to support the cause and organization with values that most closely align with their own.

Your audience has many choices of causes to support, and are drawn to those with which they are familiar. The more personable and personal you make your organization, the more it will seem familiar. Familiarity is nurtured by truthful stories, shared by ambassadors and advocates.

Your cause is bigger than your organization, and the nature of the cause is more compelling than the organization that represents it. Your organization represents the intersection of where the audience is connected with the cause, and where the audience is connected with your mission. That's why you have to be the voice.

You will always need to ask yourself: If this is our organization, what is our actual cause? Given our cause, what is our purpose? Given our purpose, what is our mission?

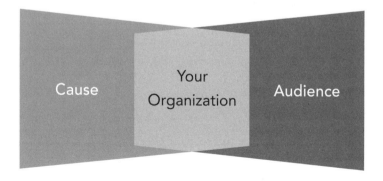

COMMUNICATING THE INVISIBLE

Intangible causes (e.g., sustainability), require data-driven messaging. The cause will draw interest by presenting the case for meeting a need to support the cause, through a rational appeal for support. When a cause (and the associated need) is tangible (e.g., children's services), direct, emotional appeals supported by data can be effective.

The trend in fundraising will continue to be to address issues rather than to simply fund programs or organizations. Fighting hunger resonates more than providing support for a food bank—but an individual's relationship may be with a local food bank. Large-scale funders will seek to address homelessness, healthcare, and many other societal issues by giving to a coalition or group of organizational partners, rather than directly funding individual organizations.

Some grant-making organizations have ascended to the perspective of funding design and communication initiatives, with the intent of empowering the nonprofit to be self-sustaining. Scalability and replication becomes increasingly important in order to achieve maximum effectiveness with this approach.

You must consider how you will communicate the invisible, as well as communicating the visible impact and outcomes. Your primary goal will continue to be one of raising awareness of the issue in addition to a secondary goal of marketing the nonprofit.

Share how your donors' gifts make an impact. Make the intangible gift of money visible through touch points that demonstrate tangible results.

WHY IMPACT IS IMPORTANT

While many things in your life maybe important, not everything can be high-priority. Such is the same with your nonprofit. Not every nonprofit or cause is a high priority to your audience, no matter how important you may think it is.

When you think about how your nonprofit shares its story, you have to think of the person on the end of the communication (otherwise, what's the point?). When the organization speaks, what do they hear? Do they respond emotionally or rationally?

The following statement's significance on the value of communications cannot be overstated:

> "Public funders—and eventually private funders as well—will migrate away from organizations with stirring stories alone toward well-managed organizations that can also demonstrate meaningful, lasting impact." MARIO MORINO, *LEAP OF REASON*

Design *and* communications are what help you demonstrate meaningful, lasting impact. Design makes stories visible. It could be that your story appeals to your supporter's heart, and how it is presented speaks to their mind.

When every nonprofit is telling a story, what will differentiate your presentation, and make it more memorable and compelling?

A powerful visual image can evoke an emotional reaction from the viewer. Even a silent, verbal voice (i.e., typography) can be effective.

Powerful voices can cut through the noise to attract

attention, but risk pushing the audience away if the tone and intensity is too high. Quiet voices can also speak powerfully, encouraging the audience to lean in to listen.

Whatever your approach, the most meaningful cause can have a powerful voice, if it understands the perspective from which it speaks.

Mission-Driven Design

"The heart may inspire you to start a journey, but you must begin with the end in mind."

I like things simple and uncomplicated. You can read books and articles, and listen to a variety of experts who speak at length about the "B" word, and in the end come away thoroughly confused. At worst, you'll leave the conversation disheartened, because branding sounds like it can be painful.

Crafting or defining a statement of purpose can be difficult, but need not be painful. If you can clearly identify your primary cause, then you can deduce your purpose. One thing that every nonprofit seems to have is a mission statement. Mission statements can be static, are often full of buzzwords, and may be best suited as an internal reminder of what your organization has set out to do. Mission statements don't make good purpose statements.

The key idea is *mission-driven* design. Driven individuals are compelled by an internal sense of urgency and conviction. Their purpose is to achieve the goals and objectives they have set before themselves. In achieving their goals, the impact may be something far greater than what they initially set out to do.

So it is also for organizations that work from a sense of purpose. What aspects of the mission *drive* you to do what you're doing? For instance, if your mission is to be a hunger relief agency that provides food resources, it's easy to deduce that your organization's higher purpose is to end hunger.

Purpose also helps you to keep focused and avoid mission creep. Your nonprofit will have many opportunities for new programs, new initiatives, and new collaborations. With new opportunities come other challenges: new funding and reporting requirements, additional staff, and less time spent doing what you do well. Staying focused on your purpose and what you're on a mission to do will enable you to say no to opportunities that don't align with your mission.

THE ELEMENTS OF MISSION-DRIVEN DESIGN

Design(ed) Thinking

Design thinking is powerful—it can help identify potential solutions to the problems faced by the nonprofit community. IDEO's free Human-Centered Design Toolkit is an excellent resource to help understand how to understand a community's needs, find innovative solutions to meet those needs, and deliver financially sustainable solutions. It can help solve your organization's communication challenges such as positioning, communication, design, media, service, and user experience.

Designed thinking is about making intentional design choices to influence interaction, experience and understanding of a meaningful cause through communication touch points that are specific to your audience. Designed thinking seeks to influence the way people think about your cause, in order to change the way they support your organization.

You may think of design and communications as branding (there's that "B" word again)—mission-driven design goes beyond branding—to focus on purpose, identity, and personality.

The most effective nonprofits manage their assets and resources according to their mission's outcomes and objectives. Those that engage their audiences most effectively communicate their purpose, mission, outcomes, and objectives. That's the mission-driven design approach.

The Definition of Mission-Driven Design

Mission-driven design is a framework that aligns design and marketing communications with the organization's purpose and mission—why it exists, and what it's on a mission to achieve. It encompasses the touch points of positioning, differentiation, strategy, design, marketing communications, media, and user experience.

Mission-driven design aligns the touch points along the Engagement Continuum to attract, inform, and inspire your audience. It helps build relationships by telling a story about your cause, and by nurturing trust in the organization that speaks for the cause.

Mission-driven design enables you to share a message—with one voice—that gives people reasons to believe in your cause, and connects your mission with your audience in a meaningful way. As relationships are formed, its role of design communications moves from engaging your audience to stewardship.

Your Positioning: You Are What They Think You Are

Mission-driven design aligns communication strategy with your organization's purpose—why it exists and why it matters. How your audience perceives your organization is determined by its positioning.

Positioning is typically an exercise in establishing how your organization is different from other similar or competing causes, organizations, and philanthropic interests.

Here are some examples of where positioning is important:

- Aside from doctrinal differences, what makes your church different from others in your neighborhood, community, or region?
- Does your audience really understand the difference between a food bank and a food pantry?
- Can site selectors quickly identify what economic development organization best represents the community or region that they are researching, when there are often similar organizations fulfilling the same role?
- If a prospective student is looking at several colleges or universities with similar degree programs, what is distinctly different about one institution that will set it apart from others (especially if the school has a reputation that does not reflect its academic culture, but its social culture)?

Powerful positioning starts from the cause and purpose of an organization and articulates the *difference* the organization makes—the measurable impact it has, and why your audience's support helps make that difference.

Your audience learns this difference through your organization's personality: its purpose, character, and culture—expressed through the touch points of print, digital, experience, and service design.

Your stated positioning—how you've articulated your purpose—should be found on your web site, in your presentations, in your literature, and in your words.

Your positioning is proven when your messaging and your audience connect. Your true positioning is realized in the place you occupy in their hearts and minds. It is created at the intersection of what you want them to think and believe about your organization, and what your audience really thinks about your organization.

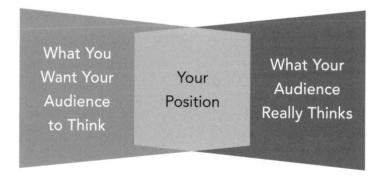

- What you want your audience to think (what you say you are) = Positioning

- What your audience really thinks (what others say you are) = Perception
- Where they intersect = Reality

This element of mission-driven design is fundamental to how your audience *perceives* your cause and your organization. You must be certain they understand who you are, what you do, why you matter, and what difference you make.

What your audience thinks about your organization is based upon what they hear and experience—through direct interaction with your organization, the media, the community, or from each other. You are not in control of what is perceived, only in control of what is expressed—the visual language and tone of voice that you choose to use.

Think of it this way: Your organization is in control of its identity, just like you are in control of yours. You control much of the way your communication appears (design and touch points); the content (messages and stories); and the manner in which it is presented (your voice).

Your audience is in control of how your organization is perceived. Their perceptions will be based on what they see, what they hear, how they hear it, and what they experience.

Perception is reality. You will need to be consistent and disciplined in projecting what you want your audience to perceive, and listen for their response. If it sounds a lot like a dialog, it is. *Communication is a conversation.*

You can own your voice and your identity—how your organization speaks on behalf of the cause it represents: the tone; the words; and the images, type, and color. You can design with purpose and seek to communicate with clarity.

THE PERSONALITY OF A CAUSE

Your personality is what makes you likable.

Your personality is the sum of all of the parts of you as an individual: your purpose in life, your character traits, your experiences, and how you express yourself.

Organizations are similar. A nonprofit's purpose is rooted in its mission and vision on behalf of a meaningful cause. Its character is based in the values that give it meaning and guide its behavior.

Its culture is defined by those values, and experienced internally and externally by its board, its staff, its supporters, and those who benefit from its programs. It expresses itself through a unique voice that is recognizable, after time, to those who have heard it before.

Your organization's personality is what makes it likable.

Purpose, character, culture, and voice should be the filter for all aspects of communications (i.e., messaging, design, storytelling, touch points, and technology). These attributes are the key to building trust; acknowledging them ensures that the voice of your cause, the stories told by your organization, and the perceptions of the audience are aligned.

Purpose

Purpose is found in the deeply held beliefs and higher calling that inspire your organization's reason for existence.

Purpose is what gives meaning to your mission. Your vision is your purpose in action.

Read your mission statement. Now think about what your true purpose is. If you asked someone outside your organization "What is our purpose?" How might they respond? Would

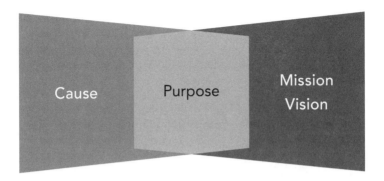

their response echo your mission, or be phrased in a different, more powerful way that echoes your organization's deeply held beliefs and higher calling?

Is your purpose associated with your cause in the mind of your audience? What are you on a mission to do? Mission must be guided by purpose so that your organization is free to say no to the things it does not do well, and yes to the opportunities that move it closer to its vision.

What is your organization's reason for being?

Here's one way to state your purpose:

- Our organization is the [x] on behalf of the cause.
- We are on a mission to do [y].
- We work to achieve [z].

Why do you need to know your purpose? Someday you might find that you need to adapt your mission to meet new needs, and what was once your vision has moved closer to reality. Your purpose will remind you of why you are the voice for your cause, and help guide your organization as it changes and adapts to a new mission.

Character

Character is found in the values that guide an organization's behavior, based on its beliefs and purpose. Values are attributes of the organization that create trust, inspire confidence, motivate action, and give credibility to its character.

What values guide your organizational behavior? Does the organization operate in a manner that is trustworthy, transparent, and accountable?

Simply put, your organization's purpose + the values that it believes in and guide its behavior = character.

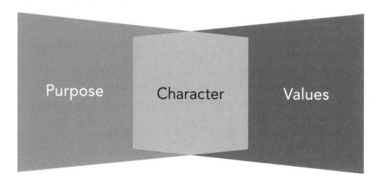

Character is something that our parents told us is built through trial and effort. It doesn't have to be built that way. The principles of the Cause Manifesto (later in this book) are values that can help you form a strategic, inspirational, relational, and aspirational character foundation.

Questions to get you thinking:
- What motivates you to achieve your mission?
- What do you stand for?
- What character qualities best represent your cause?
- What are the values that are most important to you?

Culture

Culture is the day-to-day manner in which an organization behaves and communicates its beliefs and values. Culture is character in practice, and expressed in how an organization operates. Character is revealed in how the board and leaders treat staff, volunteers, and supporters; and in every way in which the organization fulfills its purpose.

A purpose-driven culture will be guided by its mission, behave in a manner consistent with its character, focused on the cause, to the exclusion of opportunities that would be a distraction.

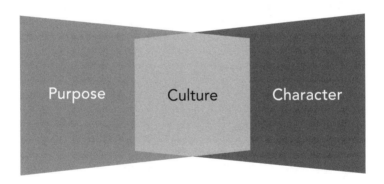

Questions to get you thinking:

- Does your culture reflect your mission?
- Does your culture reflect your organization's character?
- Is your culture transparent?
- What does your audience experience when it has the opportunity to interact with your organization?
- Does the organization appeal primarily to the audience's heart or speak to their mind?

CONNECTING WITH YOUR AUDIENCE

Your audience chooses to support the causes whose purpose, character, and culture align with their personal values and interests. Understanding their values and interests, and speaking to their motivations—with one voice—effectively engages audiences at every touch point on the engagement continuum. It's up to you to inform and inspire them in meaningful ways.

Your audience is made up of potential and current advocates, ambassadors, volunteers, supporters, and believers.

Your audience is looking for signals that tell them your cause and your organization has a purpose that is meaningful to them, and they can connect with it. They want to support a cause and volunteer in ways that give them meaning.

Your audience is looking for an organization with character it can trust. Your audience wants to *belong*—to "fit in" a culture and a community. They want to share in your experience and impact as part of the organization and as individuals.

Your audience wants a cause that they can believe in, and they want you to give them a reason to believe in you. They will believe in an organization and support the cause it represents when they learn that your values align with their values.

Your audience is listening for a voice that speaks to their minds and appeals to their hearts. They want to believe and trust in a cause that they connect with.

In becoming an organization that connects in this way, the way your cause is perceived changes. It moves from becoming a worthy cause to a meaningful cause. It becomes a cause that matters.

Of course it's always been meaningful to you, it's always been a cause that matters in your eyes.

However, a cause truly becomes meaningful when your audience says it does, and not a moment earlier. In that moment, you have become a meaningful cause that people love and believe in.

Advocates will speak on your behalf. Ambassadors will represent you wherever they go. Donors and volunteers will support you.

But believers—those who believe in your cause—will give and act and support sacrificially.

Finding Your Voice and Speaking Your Audience's Language

Through the discipline of human-focused designed thinking, you can learn to find your voice and speak your audience's language. It's essential to communicate who you are, what you do, why it matters, and the measurable impact that you have. You will want to find a way to convey your organizational personality and identity.

You want to focus on how best to communicate with your audience, and how to speak their language. You want to understand their motivations, and what messages will resonate with their values and pique their interest.

Their verbal language may be aspirational: words of the heart that attract people to your cause, and speak to how your work changes lives.

Their verbal language may be informational: numbers and data that help them see concrete results of your organization's impact.

For many organizations, it is a combination of the rational and emotional. Messages must be wrapped in stories—stories that speak to the mind and appeal to the heart. A great story creates an image in the audience's mind—words are more powerful when combined with images, typography, and color.

Mission-driven design recognizes that words are just part of the story.

- What is your audience's visual language?
- What type of images will best communicate your impact? What type of images will evoke a response from the viewer?
- Will infographics explain what your purpose is and how you achieve your mission?
- What typefaces represent your visual identity and support the tone and voice of your communication?
- How can video convey your purpose and speak to your mission?
- What color can you own, that over time will be associated with your cause or organization?

Through story and design language, your nonprofit can attract, inform, inspire, and engage its audience through marketing and communications that are focused and relevant to those who are listening.

Mission-driven design is about aligning design and communication activities to the mission; it's about creating continuity for the mission through an organization's entire culture.

When your purpose is clear, your voice is clear. Mission-driven design becomes a filter for your communication strategy, and for mission-aligned messaging that inspires ambassadors, engages your audience, and connects them with your mission.

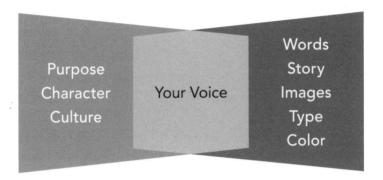

Nonprofits that follow mission-driven design principles and the Cause Manifesto find that they can speak with one voice on behalf of their cause. They are able to articulate their impact more effectively by speaking to the hearts and minds of every member of their audience: advocates, ambassadors, donors, volunteers, and more.

Mission-driven design moves your organization beyond branding to design with purpose. Intentional design choices, an understanding of how to communicate with your audience, visual and verbal continuity, and awareness of how your organization is the one voice for the cause it represents, all contribute to clarity in communications.

Remember, you're no longer thinking like a brand. You're thinking about your mission. You're thinking about design with purpose. Mission-driven design reaches beyond branding and helps position your meaningful cause in the mind of your followers. *Are you ready to raise your voice?*

Part Two

The Cause Manifesto

As I arrived for a meeting at a nonprofit where I serve on the board, one of the staff said to me, "I've been reading your blog."

I expressed my gratitude, and she mentioned the article in which these principles were first articulated as 12 communication resolutions for the New Year. She shared that she had printed out the article, and put it on her refrigerator at home.

I was humbled and surprised that these principles had resonated so deeply with her. She had printed a blog article from a web page, a numbered list of short statements. She appreciated them for their brevity and succinctness—short enough to give thought to when she walked by and read one.

The 12 principles inspired her and gave her perspective on why she was doing what she loved: working for the greater good; on staff at a regional nonprofit; and wanting to have a meaningful impact and make a difference in her community.

TIMELESS VALUES

The twelve principles of the Cause Manifesto are thought-ful insights into what I've heard expressed, over and over, in many conversations and discussions with executive directors, board members, and nonprofit professionals.

The Manifesto's principles can serve as the foundation of mission-driven design and as resolutions for improving non-profit communications.

The resolutions of the Cause Manifesto are timeless principles that align how an organization communicates its values through its purpose, character, culture, and unique voice. They speak to a higher purpose, as core values that anchor your organization's character. When put into practice, they are attributes that will make your culture stronger. Over time, they will become part of your organization's voice and help give voice to your cause.

The principles are structured around four aspects of com-munication, and the personality attributes they support:

- Strategic—purpose principles
- Inspirational—character principles
- Relational—culture principles
- Aspirational—tone of voice principles

STRATEGIC PRINCIPLES

Strategy and focus tell your audience and supporters that you know where you're headed, and how you will get there. If a cause is meaningful, it will be worth believing in.

1. **Be Strategic.** We will create and follow a road map that aligns our communications with the goals of our strategic plan.
2. **Be Focused.** We will focus our communication on one cause, one mission, and one purpose; and we will share our purpose with one voice.
3. **Be Meaningful.** We will ensure that our values and actions align with the reasons that motivate our followers and stakeholders to believe in our cause.

INSPIRATIONAL PRINCIPLES

Inspiration is achieved through visual and verbal language—design and stories—working together to create a powerful and compelling narrative.

4. **Be Insightful.** We will embrace data as a means of sharing greater insight into the outcomes of our mission, and understanding of our cause.
5. **Be Inspiring.** We will share stories that speak to the mind and appeal to the heart; these stories will reveal how our cause inspires us, and our advocates, to action.
6. **Be Engaging.** As in a conversation, we will listen as often as we speak, in order to learn what the community and our stakeholders expect of us.

RELATIONAL PRINCIPLES

Relational principles let your audience know that it's not all about you. Meaningful relationships are nurtured by gratitude and trust, with authenticity and transparency.

7. **Be Social.** We will be ambassadors for our cause, and recognize that every interaction is an opportunity to build relationships.

8. **Be Grateful.** We will express our gratitude to our supporters, remembering that their gifts are meaningful and their generosity makes a difference.

9. **Be Trustworthy.** We will seek accountability and transparency, acting and speaking in a manner consistent with our values, character, and culture.

ASPIRATIONAL PRINCIPLES

The world will continue to be changed by positive, powerful, and courageous leaders. Confident and authentic leadership will be the inspiration for their staff and supporters.

10. **Be Positive.** We will choose our words well, for they will motivate people to follow, donate, advocate, and believe in our cause.

11. **Be Powerful.** We will believe our cause is meaningful, and act in the belief that it has the power to change the world.

12. **Be Courageous.** We will dream big dreams, and have the courage to change and adapt in order to make our vision a reality.

Be Strategic.

We will create and follow a road map that aligns our communications with the goals of our strategic plan.

When counseling a business, I advise entrepreneurs and business owners to have an exit strategy, much like the thought of beginning with the end in mind. If you've planned your strategy, and have identified your outcomes, then the steps in between should be directly in line between the two. These are the tactics that get you from strategy to the completion of your goals.

If you have a strategic master plan or communication plan without tactics and actionable items, then you've simply created a wish list.

WHERE STRATEGY BEGINS

Let me start with a bold statement: **In a communication plan, branding is not a strategy.** Branding may be a priority, it may be a component of a strategic plan; but it is not a strategy.

By this time, if you agree with the framework of mission-driven design, branding is no longer part of your vocabulary, *because your cause is not a brand.*

Be Strategic. These two words should be the first words considered when determining your communication planning. They should be the first words considered with any planning.

Why be strategic? Why not just forge ahead, and hope for success?

Without a plan, mission has no focus; without focus, there is no clarity; and, without clarity, it is difficult to communicate to the outcomes that you're working to achieve.

Strategy is not an option. It is a requirement of your mission. There's a clear relationship between a strategic plan (or lack of one) and the outcomes and impact that your organization is working to achieve. Your communication plan is one bridge between a strategic plan and its execution. As you manage to outcomes, so you must create a communication plan to support the objectives and outcomes identified in the plan.

A strategic plan is the outline of goals, strategies, and tactics that guide a communications plan; that align messages with touch points; and that connect the mission with your audience.

Here's what a simple strategic communication plan might look like:

Primary Goal—e.g., Fundraising, Revenue, Awareness, Impact, Programs
- Strategy (No more than three strategies to get you to the goal)
  > An objectives statement: think of the objectives statement like a mission statement for this specific strategy. Example: *With this strategy, our objective is to accomplish [ ]. This strategy will be accomplished when [outcome], [outcome], and [outcome] are achieved.*

> 🐦 Create and follow a road map that aligns your communications with the goals of your strategic plan. #beStrategic #causemanifesto

- Tactics (No more than five specific actions that you take in order to implement the strategy. Tactics break down your strategies into short-term steps, action plans for each step, and the time frame in which to complete each step.)
  > Tactic 1 + Action Steps + Time Frame:
  > Tactic 2 + Action Steps + Time Frame:
  > Tactic 3 + Action Steps + Time Frame:
  > Tactic 4 + Action Steps + Time Frame:
  > Tactic 5 + Action Steps + Time Frame:

Each primary goal will be a complete set of the goals, strategies and tactics necessary to achieve that goal.

I recall a conversation with an executive director who remarked:

"I wish my board would let me move forward without reviewing everything I do. If a strategic plan has been completed, then the board should be behind it, since they were involved in developing it. If this is the place we need to be in five years, then what will it take to fund the plan's goals? I must be free to implement and pursue the tactics necessary to achieve the objectives."

Is this what it's like in your nonprofit board meetings, or in your relationship with the board or executive director?

STRATEGY STARTS AT THE TOP

Nonprofit staffs, busily engaged in the mission of the organization, need clear direction from the board on what is expected of them and what the goals of the organization are.

The board itself must have a clear understanding of the mission of the organization and its relation to the cause—and it must be completely certain of what the cause is and their role in the organization's purpose and fulfillment of the mission.

If the board members are believers in the organization, their actions will follow their level of commitment and belief. If they are believers in the cause, and they see the nonprofit's mission as an agent to achieve the cause, then their actions and commitment may be different. The board will have a better understanding of what is necessary and what is required to achieve the mission.

The communications plan will flow from the strategic plan. The board must empower, equip, and provide the necessary resources for the executive director or president to achieve the goals—and the resources for a communication strategy to help achieve them.

Start with the end in mind, and follow the path, communicating your progress along the way. That's how smart businesses work. That's how a strategic nonprofit should work.

KEY INSIGHTS

Strategy is not an option. It is a requirement of your mission. Without a plan, mission has no focus; without focus, there is no clarity. A communication plan without tactics and actionable items is simply a wish list.

Be Focused.

We will focus our communication on one cause, one mission, and one purpose; and we will share our purpose with one voice.

How well can you, as a board member, leader, or staff member, articulate your organization's cause and mission? Who are your primary audiences? What specific messages do you share with them?

Chances are, if you have difficulty articulating your organization's purpose (its cause and the reason that it exists), what it does (its mission), and why it matters (what difference it makes), it's possible that your organization is lacking communications focus. Let me share some examples from the higher education and technology nonprofit sector, that are relevant for any organization.

At a higher education task force meeting, I heard an excellent observation: "We can have the best programs for technology transfer and commercialization, but we can be in a room filled with business and industry executives, and none of them will have heard of the programs that we offer, what they do, how they can help—or that they even exist."

In essence, the observer could have said "Higher education

doesn't always know how to talk to business, and business isn't hearing what higher education has to say. Sometimes they don't even know we're in the same room. I feel like we're not speaking the same language."

Another example: In a college focus group, a prospective student remarked, "I know this college has lots of programs that I, and others, aren't aware of. I had to go "dumpster diving" on the web site to find the information I was looking for. The search engine didn't work effectively, and with so much other information on the web site, it was near impossible to find what I was looking for."

A harsh observation, but with a web site as the essential center of a communication ecosystem, it's an observation that should make the recruitment, marketing, and institutional advancement directors sit up and take note.

Do these two situations sound familiar to you?

Many organizations struggle to create communication and design touch points that focus on the audience. Messaging must be focused on the target audience, through touch points that *they* interact with. Web sites must be designed to meet the needs of the audience: what *they* want from your organization, and *then* what the organization wants to share with them. It's a fair exchange. You get their attention by sharing what they need to hear, and by providing information that will benefit them. In the process, they learn more about how you can help them.

In order to accomplish this, you may have to pivot. You may have to shift your focus 180 degrees.

You have to recognize that communication is not entirely about your organization's messages or stories. It's about understanding what motivates and influences your supporters, and meeting their inspirational and informational needs through those stories and your narrative. Your voice should be speaking the language they need to hear. To begin a relationship, you need to know your audience.

FIRST, IT'S A COMMUNICATIONS ISSUE

Unfocused communications are often the result of mission creep, leading to lack of focus in marketing and outreach. Mission creep may not be avoidable, but it can be manageable. If you find that you have to explain your purpose this way—"Our purpose is **X** and we are on a mission to **A** and **B** and **C** and **D**..."—you may be experiencing mission creep.

Messaging may also be diluted by communications initiatives that are sidelined by shifting priorities at the institutional, board, or executive level. You must consider the long-term sustainability of your marketing and outreach.

When any organization is trying to engage the business community (or a specific niche community), it has to be focused on that community. There must be a sustained and deliberate commitment to telling an effective story with its unique voice. The organization must remain focused on the audience it is trying to reach, speaking the language of that community.

When a nonprofit is seeking to be a credible resource and collaborator within the business community (or any other community), it has to communicate its mission and make design choices in a way that is meaningful to the audience. It must build credibility, prove itself an expert, capable of fulfilling the role it has defined for itself. It must demonstrate its competence to the specific audiences with which it wants to work. As you begin to know your audience, you will be able to identify the touch points and context that will connect with them.

In the broader picture of content, this means less focus on the organization and more emphasis on relevant content—what the audience wants to hear.

For example, when an economic development organization is seeking to attract new business and retain existing businesses, it must communicate in language that makes sense to the business community.

When your cause is seeking to attract new audiences, inform those who are interested, inspire those who are ready to take action, and engage them as ambassadors and supporters—it must communicate with the same language that the community speaks.

ELIMINATING POSSIBILITIES

To communicate effectively, you have to eliminate possibilities in order to create opportunity.

In other words, don't cast your communications net wide, unless the goal is specifically to create general awareness. Change your tactics—build relationships through appropriate touch points; attend industry events; launch a speaker's bureau; get involved with the community you want to engage in ways that are meaningful to them; create thought leadership that is the core of a content marketing program; or create a blog written from your unique point of view.

Effective communication is human-intensive. It requires focused attention and thought. Designing a program that meets the audience's informational needs is more challenging

> 🐦 Focus communications on one cause, one mission, and one purpose; share your purpose with one voice.
> **#beFocused #causemanifesto**

than a general awareness campaign. Creating a visual identity that supports a program initiative should not be a last-minute consideration.

If you are true to your goal of lasting impact, then you must take a long-term view to your design and communication planning.

To engage a specific community requires outreach that includes targeted communications touch points. In the past, traditional media may have been effective (ads in magazines and the local/regional newspapers)—but today, communications must include Twitter, LinkedIn, and perhaps even Google+. It may be different in the future; be adaptable. You need to do some research to find where your audiences are listening, and make your voice heard there.

A content marketing plan—containing content that your audience is looking for—should be created and curated. Blogs and articles about what interests your audience (as it relates to your mission), are essential resources for establishing credibility, leadership, and expertise for any nonprofit. Design the blog, white papers, and delivery mediums so they are beautiful, readable, sharable, and informational.

Your visual identity must be memorable and consistent

(but not inflexible). Design is a tool with which you communicate, so be deliberate. Remember to speak to the mind but appeal to the heart. The message need not be emotional; by making it enjoyable to read, it will be memorable.

Participate in the community by sharing information on specialized web sites that serve a specific vertical industry or community. Join conversations by contributing to groups on LinkedIn or other web sites, to build credibility as an expert in your mission-specific area of focus. Join a specialty network where your perspective and expertise about the cause will be appreciated and welcomed. Think about participating in events and creating content to draw the audience to you.

Your cause's or organization's relevance is established by participating and engaging individuals, businesses, entrepreneurs, and the community where they are—in their networks, in their LinkedIn groups, and in their associations. With a little research, you can identify and locate the best touch points and media platforms for reaching your audience.

SECOND, SPEAK THE SAME LANGUAGE: WORDS MATTER

Broad-based messaging, unless it is simply to build awareness, is not an effective method of engaging the business community. For instance, when you repeat words like *innovation* and *entrepreneur* often enough, eventually they begin to have the opposite effect of what was intended: Innovation becomes passé; and when everybody is an entrepreneur, the message is one of "all things to all people." It becomes too broad and not focused.

The key is focused messaging, delivered in the same

language that business speaks. Read *Fast Company*, *Entrepreneur*, *Forbes*, or *Harvard Business Review*; immerse yourself in the voice and tone of writers who speak the language of business everyday.

Educators speak the language of academia. The marketing department and program communications need to be the bridge, the translators, and speak the language of business.

Industry terms, as identified in curriculum (or within a program that is developed internally at an institution), are not always current (or the usage has evolved). With the rapid pace of technological advancement and the conversations around those advances, a nonprofit that serves those industries will need to be aware of the changes at every step.

Acronyms will be meaningful to your staff—but don't serve well as conversational talking points. Approach your choice of words, language, and tone of voice as if you are having an ongoing conversation with your audience.

Disruptive innovation happens at a kickstarter.com pace — rapidly and enthusiastically — whereas on the institutional level, adapting to industry changes and communicating to those changes occurs at a pace that may not keep up. Communication with the business or technology community must be in language specific to that community.

With the array of engagement tools available to any program or institution, the program needs to be on the leading edge of engagement, and not on the trailing. Get to know your audience and become familiar with the networks where they share information. Then meet them there.

THIRD, DON'T DILUTE THE MESSAGE

Messaging becomes more diluted and unfocused as it tries to demonstrate relevance of an institution's service offerings in all of its communications, and to a general audience. It should remain focused and communicate what is relevant to a specific target audience.

A quick check for broad-spectrum, unfocused messaging is this: if there is more about the institution in the messaging than there are benefits to the audience (or "what's in it for me?"), the messaging is not focused enough.

It's tough to hear, *but it's not about you!*

FOURTH, CREATE ONE POINT OF CONTACT

Organizations tend to create multiple layers to programs (funded by grants and other funding mechanisms), that by their nature create multiple and confusing entry points for anybody who is looking for help, and looking to work with the organization.

A single point of contact—a single, high-profile program or office, with a widely recognized community leader or ambassador—will be an effective engagement point for the business community. Start from a single point of contact, and resist the institutional urge to create multiple paths. At a certain point, multiple paths will even cause confusion internally, and will create obstacles to effective business community engagement.

Small nonprofit organizations should have a staff member who can respond to the information needs of your audience. A volunteer coordinator or community relations coordinator will be an effective bridge builder. Make your contact information, and the contact information for the person most likely able to help with a specific informational need, easily accessible on your web site. It should be easy for your audience to connect with your organization.

IT'S TIME TO PIVOT

If the goal is to engage the business community, communications to that audience will benefit from a pivot. Ask the business community (or whatever other community you are trying to reach) how to best communicate with them, without institutional bias—and then do it.

Think about the consumer experience (i.e., the businesses and entrepreneurs you want to reach) and then build your outreach around it. Map your audience to touch points on the engagement continuum, and you will have the foundation of a communication road map to guide you from attraction to relationships. You will have gained one more opportunity to have a meaningful conversation with the business community.

If you're courageous in doing this, you may succeed brilliantly—or you may fail spectacularly. If you fail, you'll have the insight of what doesn't work—the same insights that many entrepreneurs gain daily, and your organization will share more in common with them than ever before.

KEY INSIGHTS

Your communications have the potential to succeed spectacularly or fail spectacularly. You should never strive to fall in between. Speak the language of your audience.

Be Meaningful.

We will ensure that our values and actions align with the reasons that motivate our followers and stakeholders to believe in our cause.

Do you want to improve donor engagement? Of course you do! Imagine how it might improve if you understood how design and the donor experience impact the perception of your cause? What if you presumed that *all* communications were donor communications? How could engagement be enhanced if you made donor experience a top priority? Donors are, after all, individual people with preferences, interests and opinions.

SPEAKING TO YOUR SUPPORTER'S VALUES

Your followers choose to support causes whose purpose, character, and culture align with their personal values. Understanding and speaking to these motivations—with one voice—effectively engages donors.

Purpose, character, culture, and voice should be the filter for all aspects of communications (i.e., messaging, design, storytelling, touch points, and technology). They are the key to building trust; acknowledging them ensures the voice of your cause, the stories told by your organization, and the

> 🐦 Our values and actions will align with the reasons that motivate our followers to believe in our cause.
> #beMeaningful #causemanifesto

perceptions of the audience are aligned.

Here's a refresher on mission-driven design. Begin making your cause more approachable by answering these questions about the organization:

- What is the **cause** (e.g., education, hunger, etc.)?
- What is your organization's **purpose**? Why does your organization exist? What is your organization on a mission to do; if this is your mission, then what exactly does the organization do? Purpose must be guided by mission. (e.g., make education affordable, end hunger)
- What is your organization's **character**? Do your organization's character qualities and values flow from its purpose? What character qualities guide the organization? What values are implied by the character qualities? How do these qualities appeal to the heart of your audience? (e.g., compassion, leadership, gratefulness, innovative, etc.)
- What is your organization's **culture**? Does your organization's internal culture and external behavior align with its values? What are its motivations? How does it speak to the audience's mind? (e.g., are the organization's motivations consistent with its character and purpose?)

- What is your organization's **voice**? Does your organization speak effectively for the cause? Do your communications, activities, and interactions express the culture and character? Do all communications consistently speak with one voice? How will the organization speak? What is the tone of the communications?

KEY INSIGHTS

Be human. *The perception of your cause is based on personal, human-focused principles that clearly articulate the cause, purpose, character and culture.* Mission-driven design is the scope of strategy and communication tools with which you will reach your audience.

MISSION-DRIVEN DESIGN IS A CATALYST

With the clarity of clearly articulated core principles, mission-driven design becomes a catalyst that connects your cause with advocates, donors, volunteers, and the community. Through visual communications, interactive experiences, and relational touch points, design helps engage your stakeholders in meaningful conversations. Visual design supports consistency and creates familiarity.

Familiarity creates context, nurtures continuity and supports a culture of trust. Imagine a range of touch points that attract, inform, inspire, and engage your audience, combined with messaging that makes the case for why your cause is meaningful. These touch points include your website, publications, electronic communications, printed materials, visual identity framework, and social media. Your audience becomes familiar with your cause through consistency in experience.

A dialog with your audience through relational touch points shows that you know and understand the community, and know how to reach out to them. Continuity is created through the discipline of a consistent practice of applying your visual standards (design) and tone of voice.

THE ENGAGEMENT CONTINUUM

Experience + Engagement

ATTRACT   INFORM   +   INSPIRE   ENGAGE

STRANGERS   ACQUAINTANCES   COMMUNITY MEMBERS

VALUES ALIGNMENT TO ENGAGEMENT

As your audience sees, hears, and experiences your communication touch points, they will continue to associate your organization as the voice of the cause. When you are familiar to them, they are more likely to accept your messaging and welcome you into their lives (especially if you've shown you understand what motivates their interest in your cause). Your audience will begin to identify with your organization and seek opportunities to become a part of your community.

Design, in all formats and media, makes your stories visible. Design engages your stakeholders powerfully, from marketing and outreach to relationship building experiences and interactions.

Now do you understand that all communications are donor

communications, and must be donor-focused? How would you change your communication plan with that idea as the cornerstone?

Along with context, there must be continuity—a single voice and perspective from which your organization speaks—in championing your cause. Each interaction is an opportunity to create a lasting impression of your cause.

The next impression you make on an individual is only as good as the last impression you made; each interaction builds upon the previous one. Continuity through experience helps you build meaningful relationships, inspire trust, and motivate supporters to believe in and love your cause.

KEY INSIGHTS

Design and communications should speak to the motivation of your supporters—appealing to the mind, but speaking to the heart. Last impressions are just as important as first impressions. *How* you communicate makes *what* you communicate more powerful. How a cause is perceived is directly related to the personal interactions and experiences that individuals have with your organization.

Be Insightful.

We will embrace data
as a means of sharing
greater insight into the
outcomes of our mission,
and understanding
of our cause.

Objective insights are the knowledge, information, statistics, and observations that prove your organization is having an impact. The data you collect is just that—data.

Face it—numbers have the power to persuade and inform. Data can be your friend, and what better way to welcome a friend than to embrace her? She will help you tell your story in ways that cannot be argued against, and show you and others the results of your hard work.

WHAT'S ON THE LABEL SHOULD REFLECT WHAT'S IN THE BOTTLE

Think of your favorite product—a beverage, a household item, a food item—and what the package looks like and what's inside the package that it represents.

Whether it's a bottle, a label, or a bag, the outside of the package represents what's inside. Packaging is designed to create a perception of credibility and trust for what's inside. If the label on the package doesn't represent the contents, the buyer will be disappointed. The purpose of the packaging design is to convey trust.

Stakeholders and prospective supporters are increasingly scrutinizing the causes and organizations they support or are considering supporting. They investigate personal and relational perspectives—do they know any of the volunteers or board members? They look at independent, impersonal, and objective perspectives—financial reports, independent reviews, and what they see in news media. They read guidestar.org and charitynavigator.org for objective evaluations and ratings.

They want to be familiar with the cause and organizations they support. How have you packaged it?

Every audience perceives causes and organizations in a different way, filtering their interpretation and reception of its identity, messaging, and mission. Using all of your available data and information will help you create messaging that informs, speak to impact, and progress toward outcomes.

Think of it this way: You understand your organization's character, purpose, mission, and culture. Your goal is to help your audience understand it in the same way you do in order to create a connection.

DATA IS AN OBJECTIVE, IMPARTIAL INDICATOR OF AN ORGANIZATION'S PURPOSE

What statistical data is relevant to your story? What is the best way of sharing that information with your stakeholders, so they understand and experience how effective you are in advancing the cause? What must you communicate in order to create advocacy and support for the outcomes you're seeking to achieve?

> 🐦 Data will help us tell our story and gain greater knowledge and insight into the outcomes of our mission.
> #beInsightful #causemanifesto

In the same way an organization must manage to outcomes, mission-driven design choices show you're communicating about how you are achieving those outcomes.

Have you seen Dan Pallotta's thought-provoking TED talk? *The way we think about charity is dead wrong* (http://ow.ly/qI5Pm) challenges the thinking behind funding for communications and marketing in the context of program delivery and overhead.

Pallotta remarks: "Too many nonprofits are rewarded for how little they spend—not for what they get done." He suggests that we start rewarding charities for their goals and accomplishments, and that marketing and communication are an essential programming expense. Data and information are tools that you can use to prove what you get done.

Data and information—from the numbers on an organization's Form 990, to social media messages, to research and reports from initiatives—matters. Some of the data you should be interested in is qualitative: internal and external feedback, observations, and insights based on circumstances or experiences. Some of the data you should be interested in is quantitative: numbers and statistics; budgets, revenues and expenses; polling data; and program metrics.

Whether it's qualitative or quantitative, paying attention

to data (you can also call it information) means you're *listening*. When you're listening, that means you're paying attention to the outcomes and results of your purpose and mission.

Information is knowledge that can help guide and give insight to mission-driven design choices and communications. Data can be the foundation of a very compelling story.

VOLUNTEER INSIGHTS — EXPERIENCE IS DATA

A volunteer's experiences will reflect the culture, quality of communications, and value placed on their service.

The tendency in any organization is to look at activities from the inside out, but the problem with this is you can't see or experience it as an outsider does. In essence, you can't see the label if you're on the inside of the bottle.

Volunteers not only perceive an organization from an outside perspective; but, because of the nature of what they do, they also form a perception based on their internal volunteer experience. This is why it's so critical that the external behavior and character of an organization accurately reflect the internal experience.

- Volunteers help advance the cause and are part of the narrative of the organization. They are participants in achieving the cause.
- Volunteers are ambassadors for the cause and contributors to the mission of the nonprofit organization.
- How effectively an organization communicates with volunteers indicates the level of respect it has for them.
- Volunteering is as much about the cause as it is about the feeling one gets while serving.

- A volunteer believes their contribution is meaningful and that it adds value to their life.

OUTSIDE OBSERVATIONS

From independent reviews of your nonprofit's performance, to suggestions for monitoring how your organization and the cause it represents is perceived, here are several outside perspectives to which you should pay close attention:

- Charity Navigator: charitynavigator.org
- GuideStar: guidestar.org
- Better Business Bureau Wise Giving Alliance Standards for Charity Accountability: bbb.org/charity-reviews
- Social media: Not only should an organization have a plan for social media, it should be monitoring its engagement on Twitter, Facebook, LinkedIn, and other platforms. Hootsuite, Twitonomy, and other social media management tools are essential resources for management and monitoring.
- Klout: klout.com
- TV and newspapers: Media reports will be more accurate when the board and the executive leadership can articulate the nature of the cause, and the mission of the organization.

KEY INSIGHTS

Paying attention to data means you're *listening*. When you're listening, that means you're paying attention to the outcomes and results of your purpose and mission.

Be Inspiring.

We will share stories
that speak to the mind
and appeal to the heart;
these stories will
reveal how our cause
inspires us, and our
advocates, to action.

WHAT DOES IT MEAN TO BE INSPIRING?

Words inspire us. How they are designed and how they are delivered can make them more meaningful and more powerful. The right words, shared at the right time, give meaning to individuals and groups who have an affinity for your cause. Words create an expectation of reality; anticipation for what is promised, hope for what is to come.

To be inspiring is to cast a vision for what the future will be, and how that future will be realized through the mission of your organization.

Words are powerful elements of alignment: key themes and messaging must be carefully selected and crafted to create a memorable perception of your organization and the cause it represents. The words and phrases that are chosen (such as the positioning statement, the tag line and words that represent the values, character, and attributes of the cause) are the phrases that you want your followers and advocates to share and to use in conversation about the cause.

Ambassadors should know what to say, and how to say it inspirationally.

Words—combined with powerful typography and memorable imagery—evoke meaning, motivate people to action, and become a catalyst that leads to changed thinking in the minds (and hearts) of those you're seeking to engage.

Changed thinking leads to changed behavior. Change the perception of the cause (how your supporters think about it), and you'll change the behavior of the supporter.

Consider the example of an independent economic development organization that represents a Midwest county. Our research revealed (and was validated by post-visit surveys), that site selectors characterized the county as a lazy, backwards, rust-belt region of the country. To project a positive perception of the county (and after research into what site selectors are looking for in a locale),

> Does your board orientation include a session to inspire the new directors?

we chose the phrases "welcoming, hard working, forward thinking, progressive, and vibrant."

Herein lies the power of words: as the economic development organization integrated these positive phrases into their marketing and presentations, perceptions began to change. This was most evident when the post-visit surveys show that site selectors were now beginning to use those same words in their descriptions of the county and how they described *their* visit.

Every interaction—words that are read, spoken, or heard—must be positive and encourage participation in the future that is promised and the change to which your organization aspires. Inspiring words convey *hope*.

> 🐦 Share stories that speak to the mind and appeal to the heart. **#beInspiring #causemanifesto**

Even your visual identity must be inspiring. It should represent what you aspire to become and the community that you are inviting your supporters to belong to.

To inspire is to stir the heart and challenge the mind of a follower. When an individual understands that their values align with your organization's values and the cause it represents, their participation gives them more than an opportunity to be involved. It gives them a story to share, a point of connection, and personal meaning.

Your organization must be inspiring, because people want a cause to believe in. Choose your words well and they will motivate people to follow, donate to, advocate for, and *believe in* your cause. Inspire them, and they will be motivated and engaged. Inspire them and they will become more than advocates and donors—they will become believers in the cause.

The first place to instill the sense of inspiration is in the board of directors—those individuals who have committed, first and foremost, to the success of the organization. They must be the ambassadors that believe whole-heartedly in your cause. Does your board orientation include a session to inspire the new directors to inspire others?

Why are believers important? Volunteers and donors will give of their time and money, advocates will be engaged in

promoting the cause—but believers will give and serve sacrificially. Believers become ambassadors, who will represent your
organization wherever they are, because their values align
with the cause. Believers will follow wherever the organization leads, and will support your cause when you've inspired
them to action. Your inspiration gives them meaning because
they are part of the change and impact.

The world is watching, and it is asking: *"Do you want me to
follow? Inspire me!"*

KEY INSIGHTS

*Design inspires. It makes your mission visible, and connects
the cause with the heart and mind.* Mission-driven design
is personal, human-focused design. It enables your
organization to share many messages with one voice, for
one purpose, about one cause, in a manner that is most
meaningful to the donor.

Be Engaging.

As in a conversation,
we will listen as often
as we speak, in order to
learn what the community
and our stakeholders
expect of us.

Have you ever had this kind of conversation?

"Hello, how are you?"
"Fine, thanks."

And that's where it ends? It's as if you wanted to play catch, and threw somebody a ball—only to have the person hold the ball and not throw it back.

Being engaging isn't always about sharing the great things you're doing. Sometimes you need to ask your audience what they think, in order to find the points of interest where they want to have a conversation with your organization. People are always interested in talking about themselves!

When was the last time you asked your audience:

- "What do you expect of us?"
- "What is your experience with us like?"
- "Why do you support our cause?"

Have you contacted your major funders recently and asked them "Are you satisfied with the impact of your investment?" Have you asked them how *they* are doing?

What do you think might change if you asked your major donors these questions and discussed these statements?

- What is the most effective way we can communicate with you?
- How many times in a year would you like to hear from us?
- Are there any changes in your grantmaking policies that we need to be aware of?
- From your perspective, are we meeting the needs of the community through our programs?
- Do you think we could have greater impact through collaboration or a more focused application of grants?
- We see the value of including design and communications expenses as part of the program funding for which we're requesting grants. What is your opinion on that perspective?
- We think we can become more sustainable and effective by increasing awareness of our cause. Would you consider providing support for a communications plan that aligns with our programs?

The last two discussion points will perhaps be the most awkward to discuss. Many supporters and funders still see design and communications as capacity building or overhead expenses. In reality, they are a critical component of program delivery.

This is where nonprofits need to engage their enlightened supporters and funders in an honest conversation about the

> 🐦 Listen as often as you speak,
> to hear what the community is saying.
> #beEngaging #causemanifesto

value of design and communications as program support—not overhead.

Strategic grantmaking is the preference of the specific funder or philanthropy, but to create and fund a program without a supporting design and communication strategy is like building a stool with only two legs. You can't expect great results and impact without committing to a complete investment.

A challenge to the board: How many directors own a business or are an executive of a corporation? Think about your own firm's marketing budget, and compare it to what the nonprofit you govern has budgeted for design, communications, and fundraising. Most likely, the figure is much less than one percent of the overall budget.

How do you expect great results if you're unwilling to make an investment in communicating to the results you expect to achieve?

DAY-TO-DAY ENGAGEMENT

Interacting with your audience happens at a very practical level as well, on a day-to-day basis. Processes, technology, volunteer experience, and donor experience should all be evaluated from your audience's perspective. What works well for the organization may be a miserable experience for your audience.

I'm a big advocate for user experience (UX). You may be familiar with UX—it's how people interact and experience something, whether it's software, an event, or any other user interaction.

Designing user experience not only builds affinity for your organization and the cause, it can also have a profound effect on your staff and culture. It shows that you're thinking about what matters to your audience and your staff.

Think about every possible touch point between your nonprofit and its audience. What could you do to improve these interactions? First, ask your audience for feedback, and then ask your staff as well.

Here are two very practical examples that touch the staff and the donors:

Making Time for More Service

Every year in November, the inbound call volume at Second Harvest Food Bank of North Central Ohio would begin to rise. Individuals and families would call the Food Bank looking for information about where to find emergency food assistance.

The volume of inbound calls reduced the amount of time that staff could attend to other business, such as agency relations, and sourcing and shipping food.

Recognizing how critical it was to solve the problem, the board approved and funded a new web site that included a transformational component: a directory of food pantries, soup kitchens, and hot meal programs that could be searched on mobile and desktop devices.

The directory can be searched by type of program, city, county, and zip code. Once the results are delivered, the search results reveal the date, time and location of the resource.

This is significant—the nature of food pantries is they are often hosted at faith-based organizations that rely on volunteers. The dates and times a pantry is open can vary widely (e.g., the second Thursday from 11 am to 1 pm; and the third Wednesday from 10 am to 2 pm).

This solution came from listening to what staff felt would help them to more effectively do their jobs and meet the needs of the hungry, by providing direct access to the resource. The food assistance portal is consistently the second-most visited section of the Food Bank web site.

Listening to Donor Experience Improves Online Giving

If engagement is a dialog, how closely are you listening? In order to make the case for the cause, you must adapt to the needs of the audience; don't expect the audience to adapt to you. Listening closely to stakeholders enables you to influence the way individuals perceive your cause and interact with it.

Historical giving data revealed that individual donations were a growing portion of funds raised by Second Harvest Food Bank of North Central Ohio. Research from GivingUSA.org backed up this data. However, donors constantly commented that online giving was difficult and frustrating. This was due to several factors:

- Second Harvest's online donation platform was a third-party ecommerce platform, better suited for product sales than online donations.

- Donors were forced to leave the parent web site, which diminished trust in Second Harvest and created a disruptive, instead of a seamless experience.
- The ecommerce platform required the donor to set up a user account—a step that became a barrier to the donor's desire to make a contribution.
- The platform offered limited options for customizing the appeal to the donor's interest in giving (to support a specific program or campaign). This prevented Second Harvest from asking for the donation with confidence.

Rather than feeling good about impacting a specific area of hunger relief, what the donor remembered most was the difficulty of donating. The gift-giving experience was less meaningful than it should have been and potentially contributed to a negative perception of Second Harvest.

It is acknowledged within the fundraising community that donors give because they are asked, and because it makes them feel good. If you start from that perspective with your fundraising appeals, you can listen for other influences and motivations, and refine your appeals as you learn.

Because of this feedback, Second Harvest made major changes to its online donation process:

- Second Harvest chose a new payment processor and integrated donation forms into their web site; as a result, donors welcomed the opportunity to give without being redirected off-site.
- Second Harvest customized their appeal pages to match the donation form with the program that the donor is interested in supporting.

- Second Harvest enhanced their generic appeal page with an image of impact—individuals who would benefit from the donation—to remind donors that their gifts impact people, not programs.
- To gain insights, a single question was added to the donation form: "Why do you support Second Harvest?" It's humbling and revealing to read the responses, especially the one that read, "Because I was poor once."

KEY INSIGHTS

Engagement is a conversation that gives your audience the reasons to believe in your cause. Giving is meaningful to donors, but the ease of giving is as important to them as the satisfaction they receive after giving. Leadership must have the courage to change established procedures, even if it means changing how donations are processed, and in the way requests for funding are made. In particular, your technology must adapt to how donors interact with it; you should never expect donors to adapt to your process or technology. True engagement considers the needs of the audience first.

Be Social.

We will be ambassadors for our cause, and recognize that every interaction is an opportunity to build relationships.

There is a groundswell of well-intentioned, but unfounded faith in social media as the cure-all for a lack of mission-driven design discipline. This is particularly true for organizations that have grown so large that they suffer from undiagnosed mission creep. It is also popular as a topic of discussion at conferences that seek to educate the nonprofit and higher education sectors. Technology and social networks will never replace personal interaction, one-to-one relationships, and authenticity in storytelling. As with any relationship, you can't be social without knowing your audience.

If an organization lacks clear mission focus, its communications will be unfocused. Social media is often seen as the way to target the masses and hope for results.

Here's what you may not realize: *All media is social media.*

That's brilliant, right? It's also a blatant display of the obvious. What is social can be shared: conversations, printed literature, experiences, events, memories, and more.

Online services may help to build community; they can

be an effective way to leverage an interpersonal social network. But they are, and always will be, part of the relationship mix—just one of many touch points and design choices available to help your organization communicate better.

Social media, like any other touch point, requires a strategic, focused plan based on the design, marketing, and communication objectives. Not only must the editorial aspects of social media planning be considered; so too must the tools that will enable the cause's followers to share the stories.

Sharing tools can help ambassadors. Ambassadors include the board of directors, the staff, and stakeholders (those who receive services from the organization or institution), volunteers, donors, advocates, grantmaking organizations, the media, and legislators. Do you see? Everybody is a potential ambassador. How have you equipped them to be able to share your story in a manner that is meaningful to them?

MESSAGE, STORY, AND AUTHENTICITY
- "Keep your story straight."
- "Stay on message."
- "These are the talking points."

Each of these phrases is more about presentation than about practice. Words can be rehearsed; conversations can be practiced; speakers can be prepped for what they will say. What truly resonates with an audience is authenticity. Ambassadors and advocates should be familiar with their content, so it can be delivered in a way that is natural, confident, sincere, and uplifting.

Core messages aren't stories. They are the foundation upon which stories can be created, and serve as the filter for what stories support the organization's purpose. Core messages are built upon facts and information, formed from the purpose for which the organization exists, and are the elements of truth that will inform your audience.

Stories are what inspire your audience. Good storytelling can come from a variety of sources—from those who are impacted by your work, testimonials from your audience, and everyday experience in delivering programs and services. Good stories have the potential to touch the heart and motivate listeners to action.

Stories can be truthful or fictional. We've all read fiction, heard fairy tales, and certainly have had a nonprofit represent itself through fictionalized stories. We've heard speakers embellish the truth of the message with facts we later find to misrepresent the truth.

Simply reciting core messaging and telling second-hand stories is not authentic. You can't fake authenticity and sincerity. As an ambassador and advocate, there comes a point at which *how* you act and behave, and how you speak and listen, flows from within. Either you believe in the cause and the purpose for which your organization exists, or you're faking it.

Communications begin with core values. Consider the Manifesto as a set of guiding principles, in setting the tone for your organization's voice and how it communicates through every touch point.

Every piece of literature, every communication tool—from its collateral to its web site—could benefit from the perspective of core principles to help guide messaging toward authenticity.

> As ambassadors, we recognize that every interaction is an opportunity to build relationships. **#beSocial #causemanifesto**

Likewise, those who are in the role of ambassadors for their organization would benefit from principles that help them set the tone for how they deliver the core message.

It's imperative any communications follow principles that uphold the values of the organization or institution. Those who are in the role of ambassador are obligated to put the cause first, and understand how their words and the communication toolkit are designed to support that cause.

The resolutions of the Manifesto are a set of guiding principles that can enhance your organization's ability to speak with one voice. When your audience hears one voice that supports your purpose, character, and culture, the outcome is verbal and visual design continuity, and a culture of authenticity, accountability, transparency, and trust. Think of an orchestra—many instruments under the direction of a conductor—blending into a cohesive performance, unified by the theme, and yet interesting because of its variations.

Your voice—and the touch points that appeal to our ears, eyes, and minds—must be as carefully guarded as spoken words.

The truth of authenticity is always revealed in the expression of an ambassador who is speaking on behalf of a cause.

The written word gives the writer the luxury of review. Speaking engagements can be scripted (designed) and planned; and, where possible, allow minimal opportunity for off-the-cuff remarks.

Those in positions of authority and leadership have a responsibility to their cause and their constituents. The way we think is shown by our actions; our words express what is in our heart.

Action reveals thought and words reflect the heart. What we believe, and what motivates and inspires us, is eventually revealed through words and actions.

The Heart and Mind of an Ambassador

When you are an ambassador, you live your life as a representative of the cause. When your words flow from believing in the purpose, and with the conviction of character values that define the organization, you embody its culture.

You believe your cause has the power to change the world. You believe the core message points are true and speak them from the heart, because your mind has acknowledged that they are true. You become part of the narrative and express your experience from your own perspective.

You become an example of one who has moved from being a follower to a *believer* that will live and give sacrificially.

This Is Who We Are

We are all ambassadors. As an ambassador, you can pretend to believe in the cause, or you can live with purpose.

If you are involved with any nonprofit that represents a cause that matters, then you are an ambassador. And since you are an ambassador, it's up to you to represent the cause well, be aware of your role, and be authentic.

SOCIAL EVENTS

Many cause-related fundraising activities, particularly donor cultivation and acquisition, have event-driven components. Many fundraising events involve vast amounts of time, volunteer and staff commitment, planning, and resources. At the end of the event, many organizations realize that the return on their investment, in terms of actual dollars raised, was not worth the time and effort involved.

Many organizations will excuse this low ROI and claim that the event raised awareness of the cause, even if it didn't raise the amount of money that was intended. If this is the case, then wouldn't the investment of time, effort, and financial resources been better spent on an awareness-building campaign that had the potential to reach hundreds, if not thousands, more individuals?

Consider this example of an international organization that sought to improve donor cultivation. The organization hired a consulting firm that recommended a strategy of donor cultivation that focused on high-value potential donors. Its process pre-qualified them before inviting them to a friend-making event, where an appeal would be made to contribute to the organization and support the cause.

This approach focused on building a relationship, over time, with potential donors who had an expressed interest in, and motivation for, making a gift. The approach was very effective, resulting in larger donations that fueled the growth of the organization.

Yet at the same time, it became more and more challenging to sustain the level of giving needed to maintain the requirements of the organization as it grew. The goal of the strategy was creating sustainable funding for the cause, but the organization was allowed to grow in an unsustainable way because of the increase in income. The strategy did not realize the intended effect of creating a stewarded resource of donors. Instead, it created a small pool that quickly reached the limit of its engagement and donation capacity.

Why was this strategy flawed? One perspective suggests it was the apparent lack of sustained continuity. It appeared that the engagement continuum was followed:

Attract > Inform > Inspire > Engage

But the continuity aspect of the engagement continuum was missing:

Attract > Inform > Inspire > Engage > *Steward*

Mission-driven design recognizes the ultimate goal isn't to cultivate or acquire donors, it is to *build relationships* and *create ambassadors and believers* in your cause. Donors will give if they are asked. *Believers* will support your cause sacrificially, and often without being asked—out of generosity rather than duty. *Ambassadors* will represent your organization and advocate for the cause wherever they go.

This is where the difference between nonprofit marketing and communications is most distinct. On the engagement continuum, marketing decreases while relationship building increases.

THE ENGAGEMENT CONTINUUM

Experience + Engagement

ATTRACT   INFORM   +   INSPIRE   ENGAGE

STRANGERS   *MARKETING DECREASES >*   COMMUNITY MEMBERS

ACQUAINTANCES

RELATIONSHIP BUILDING INCREASES >

VALUES ALIGNMENT TO ENGAGEMENT

Marketing touch points are intended to attract the most attention possible, and draw people into the engagement continuum. How you inform and inspire them are mission-driven design choices, and require information and storytelling in order to build credibility and be effective. As individuals move through the continuum, the touch points are more personal and meaningful. They may take the form of traditional media, but their content needs to speak to the mind and appeal to the heart—according to how these individuals are motivated, and how their values align with your cause. Your supporters start off as strangers; become acquaintances; and, when they become engaged and active, grow into community members. Some will move through the entire continuum and become believers, having been stewarded in their relationship with your organization.

Ask people to do more, and they will. Understand what inspires and motivates them, and you will be astounded at how much more they will do when it is meaningful to them. You just have to ask.

MEASURING SOCIAL MEDIA

At some point, the idea of *being social* returns to social media, which are actually digital social networks. A board member, CEO, or president will ask "How do we measure our social media engagement," or "How do we know this is worthwhile?"

Many articles and papers have been written about measuring the ROI and ROE of social media. The idea of socially sharing one's life and interests is

> Look for thoughtful resources and perspectives on social media for nonprofits at causemanifesto.com.

not going away. Individuals—especially the millennial generation—love to share what's meaningful and important in their lives. Judging from the number of food and clothing photos one sees, it's the day to day that is meaningful as well. Perhaps there's a lesson to be learned in that observation.

Think of ROI as the *Return on Influence* of social media. Think of ROE as the *Return on Engagement*. ROE and ROI are closely related: What is the best way to measure your engagement with advocates and your influence on them? How can you measure their influence on and engagement with your organization?

Of course, if you're skeptical, you're not going to be convinced that your social media influence is measurable or worthwhile. You'll only see how effective it can be as a supplement to your communication strategy once you try it. Search online and you'll find a wealth of resources about ROI and ROE in social media.

Engagement is how you measure the level of interaction you're having with your audience. Influence is the measure of the reach those interactions have.

For example: You may be reading this book as a result of a referral, social media post, or tweet. (Of course, I am deeply flattered if you are reading it!) If you've read this far, you're obviously engaged in the book. If you do nothing but read it, it's neither possible to measure the book's influence, nor can I measure its engagement in social media. If you share it with your followers, then I can measure the influence of the book, as well as my engagement with you and your followers, especially if you share thoughts using the suggested hash tags. (Have you noticed the "key insights" at the end of every principle chapter?)

Engagement Is Interaction; Interaction Is Conversation

Engagement is an indicator of how well you are interacting with your audience. In social media measurement analytics, you'll be able to see exactly what posts were shared, interacted with, or noted as a "favorite." Measuring your engagement in some manner is a key indicator of how well you're both listening to and conversing with your audience. The interaction with your audience builds relationships, affinity, and loyalty—which leads to influence.

Influence Is Interest; Interest Leads to Action

Is your audience interested? Influence is indicated by the growth of your followers across social media platforms, and by your audience's level of interest in what you're sharing. Simply put, influence is measured by the number of followers you have, how they share your posts, and the extent to which they share your content.

It's a virtuous cycle; engagement and influence work together as in a face-to-face relationship. As you express interest in your audience, they respond and express interest in you, and relationships continue to be built.

KEY INSIGHTS

All *media is social media*. What is social can be shared, in conversation, online and in print. Measure what you can. *Action reveals thought and words reflect the heart*. What we believe, and what motivates and inspires us, is eventually revealed through words and actions.

Be Grateful.

We will express our gratitude to our supporters, remembering that their gifts are meaningful and their generosity makes a difference.

BUSINESS AS USUAL

I've attended different local churches all of my life. My wife and I recently started attending a church minutes from our home. To our surprise, we received a personal thank you from this church for a donation we made in addition to our regular giving. The regular practice for a church is to send a year-end letter acknowledging financial donations. Most likely, the letter is generated as a form letter, personalized (but not personal), and sent in a #10 envelope.

My wife and I consider ourselves to be generous people. We support meaningful causes. We think of money as a means to bless others. We volunteer and hold leadership positions where we serve. We think of our time and talents as more valuable than money. We've received personal thank you notes from other organizations after we made a donation, but this was the *first* instance that we received such a note from a church for a gift we had made.

It was both wonderful and unsettling.

It was wonderful because we were on the receiving end of gratitude and sincere thankfulness. Our gift was as meaningful to the church as it was to us.

It was unsettling, because it made me realize that other churches we had attended considered our giving as a duty, where a year-end form letter was sufficient.

Our values are such that we volunteer and support the causes we believe in with a generous spirit, not from a sense of duty. We give because it is meaningful to us and we believe in the cause—not because it is expected. We want to support the organizations that speak on behalf of the causes we believe in.

Of course, it would be a logistical challenge for a church that relies on weekly giving to send out a thank you note every week—*or would it?* How could it powerfully transform the connection the donor has to their church and the cause it represents, if gratitude were expressed every week?

I am proud to have served for many years on the board of Second Harvest Food Bank of North Central Ohio. I am always impressed that *every* donor receives a personally signed thank you card, for every donation that is made. The notes are sent because the gift was meaningful to the donor, and the thank you note is an acknowledgment that the gift is meaningful to the Food Bank.

Small actions often speak louder than big words. A thank you note leaves an impression that will last for years. The most recent impression you make may be the most memorable.

ACTIONS SPEAK LOUDER THAN WORDS

It's not always what you say, it's often how you say it. Consider again that all communications are donor communications.

You may be thinking that there is a question of scale—not every donor is an individual, and not every donation can be acknowledged in the same way. What about grants? What about major gifts? What about capital campaigns? Every gift must be acknowledged, and never ignored. The acknowledgment should be appropriate to the gift. Some gifts warrant thank you notes or letters. Larger gifts might warrant a personal call or letter from the executive director or a board member. Transformational gifts might require that you name a building, or offer another form of personal recognition.

> A colleague shared: "When I get busy and need to refocus, I write thank you notes."

Ask the supporter why they are making the gift, and what it means to them. Ask them what they might be expecting in return (if anything). Never assume anything. You won't know what their true motivation is until you ask—whether it's altruistic or for seeking personal recognition—or somewhere in between.

You won't know a supporter's specific motivation until you ask. If you ask, you will be able to express the organization's gratitude for the gift in a way that is most meaningful to the donor (and you'll be able to gather relevant data as to why your supporters get involved with and donate to your cause).

Regardless of the type of donation, every donation must be acknowledged. It's not about whether it's convenient for your organization, or if there is no process in place. Being grateful is a principle that acknowledges to your supporters that their gifts are meaningful. Gratefulness recognizes that the gift is important and will make a difference. Being grateful is about how the donor feels about giving, not about the gift itself. Gratefulness is a cultural practice.

HOW WOULD YOU FEEL?

Let me share another story with you, about why being grateful matters.

During the course of a project, my firm chose to make a gift-in-kind donation of services for the program with which we were working. We recognize the importance and value of the mission of the program, and are fully committed to the cause it represents.

The project on which we were working was extensive; a significant change in scope went beyond the budget that had been approved, and for which we would be paid. We chose to continue our work and complete the project on a pro bono basis, with the intent to report the work as a gift-in-kind donation.

The goal was to enhance the perception of the program as a leader in its area of influence, and we felt compelled to contribute to that goal. By all measures, the project was a success, and improved the perception of the program to its stakeholders (including a major grantmaking organization)—not only regionally, but also nationally.

As is our policy, and at our client's request, we wrote a letter outlining our gift-in-kind donation, and explained our decision to make the equivalent of a five-figure contribution of strategic and creative services. The program office acknowledged receipt of the letter, and forwarded a copy to the parent organization for recording of the donation.

Then we waited.

One, two, three weeks went by. I started thinking that it was unusual that we had not received even a simple acknowledgment of the contribution. We considered our gift to be an important and significant contribution. We waited one more week, and in the fifth week reached out to the program office to inquire as to whether or not our letter was even received by the parent organization.

As it turned out, neither the parent organization staff nor the leadership seemed to be aware of the donation—or the letter. A short while later we received what was clearly a form thank you letter, with a computer-generated signature of the parent organization's president. Most likely, the individual is still unaware of our gift.

Needless to say, I was disappointed. I understand our gift was not monetary. What was a meaningful, generous gift of services was absorbed into the organization without consideration.

The thank you became meaningless, and my affinity for and belief in the cause changed that day.

A relationship that had been stewarded and nurtured over many years was tarnished by the oversight of something as simple as recognition and acknowledgment of this donation. The leadership did not recognize the significance of the donation to my business, and my family, as the donor. Not only do I have the perception that the gift was not meaningful to them, but in my mind the perception was also created that they did not recognize it was meaningful to me.

Do you have a similar story in your life where the expectation of gratefulness was met with indifference?

It doesn't have to be this way.

We also support a different nonprofit through design and marketing services. The relationship with this organization had become one in which I thought our gifts of time and resources were unappreciated and taken for granted. A newly-appointed leader of this organization specifically called to ask if we would be willing to continue our support, instead of assuming that we were still interested. He took the time to meet with me and explain that our help was crucial to their cause, and asked if we would be willing to continue our work. Since then, I've received thank you notes and verbal acknowledgments of appreciation for the work we've done. This leader recognized that our gifts are meaningful and, through his expressions of gratitude, reminded me that they are appreciated. *That's the way it should be.*

A SACRED TRUST

Gratefulness is a sacred trust: donors *choose* to support organizations whose purpose upholds the values they hold most important, and whose mission they believe in. Gratefulness is a character quality, and is expressed in the culture of your organization.

The values that represent a cause are expressed in the character of your organization. Organizations have purpose, expressed through their character and acted on through their culture.

Donors and supporters entrust you with their values through the donation of time or money or services. What you

> 🐦 We are grateful, and recognize our supporters' gifts are meaningful and make a difference. **#beGrateful #causemanifesto**

do with it, how you hold the trust sacred, how you acknowledge it—sends a message about how meaningful their gift is. When a gift is not acknowledged or service is not recognized, you're not just demeaning a donor's gift, you're rejecting their values.

Philanthropy, development, and stewardship would be transformed if every advocate, ambassador, and fundraiser understood the true gift that is given is the supporter's trust. Money, services, or time is an accompaniment to that gift, and evidence of the donor's commitment.

Fundraising relationships will be transformed when you realize what you are asking a donor to do is trust you to manage their investment for a measurable impact. Money, or any other gift, is just proof of the exchange.

The trust a supporter gives an organization is more important than the donation that accompanies it.

STEWARDSHIP

Even if a gift or donation isn't meaningful to the organization—it's always of primary importance to the donor. How it is acknowledged will affect the relationship forever. Every gift or act of support comes with the supporter's hope and expectation of making an impact. Acknowledging the impact that the gift has made, or will make, is essential to stewardship.

The fact that our in-kind donation was overlooked may have been an oversight; it may have been a breakdown in process; it may be that there is no process at all. In any organization, there should be a clearly defined process in place—from the board, to the executive level, to the fundraising level, to the staff—a policy and process of what must occur when any donation is made.

Think about any organization you are involved with. Are you aware of what occurs after a donation is made? How a nonprofit responds after a donation is made is critical to the stewardship of the donor relationship.

STEWARDSHIP STARTS AT THE BEGINNING

Consider the many types of tax exempt entities who accept donations: churches, charities, foundations, colleges, universities, and schools. Each accepts donations of different monetary amounts, and in different ways. In churches and faith-based organizations there is an expectation of giving. Based on interpretation of religious doctrine, a percentage is anticipated. At times, a church member's commitment to the cause may even be evaluated based on that percentage.

Colleges and universities solicit funding from alumni and the community—communicating the core values of the institution, in order to project values that align with these stakeholders. Their marketing and outreach also seeks to appeal to potential supporters' interest in education, economic development, athletics, research, the arts, or any other initiative that the institution has as part of its mission.

Foundations seek gifts to create impact-based grants, awarding support to charities and meaningful causes that apply for funding from the foundations, the community, and individuals.

We tend to see gratitude as a one-time activity that is accomplished once a thank-you note is sent. But when it comes to stewarding donors, why not consider it as an ongoing process? Never pass up an opportunity to say thank you and engage a donor at a deeper level.

- Gratefulness must be part of your tone of voice in all communication touch points.
- Volunteers must be affirmed and thanked for the gift of their time in support of your cause, no matter where, when, or how they serve. All volunteer time is important, don't take any of it for granted.
- Begin the process of thanking every individual in the same way you thank institutional grant-making donors. A personally signed thank you from the executive director, president, or CEO is meaningful, and greatly appreciated by any donor. Sign it in a different color of ink to show its authenticity.
- Reach out to advocates and engage them enthusiastically in social media. Have a conversation. Say thank you. Ask questions.

Think of your own experience:

- What frame of mind are you in when you are likely to make a donation? What are your expectations once the donation is made?

- Are you expecting a thank you?
- Is email sufficient?
- Would a personal note be more meaningful?
- Would a personal phone call make you feel that your donation really mattered?

The largest of national and regional nonprofits will have mostly automated processes for acknowledging donations; these will be personalized as much as possible and will project the appearance of personalization. There are an abundance of local nonprofits, from charities to churches to colleges, that could benefit from truly personalized expressions of thanks, appropriate to the size and type of donation.

> A personal thank you says *"We appreciate your donation. We're thankful that our mission is important to you, and that you want to support the cause we represent. We are committed to be good stewards of your donation, and our ongoing relationship with you is as meaningful as the investment you have made in us."*

When an individual understands how their values align with your organization's values and the cause it represents, their participation and support gives them more than an opportunity to be involved—it gives them a story to share; a point of connection; and personal meaning. Supporters of all types want to be invited into a relationship (attracted); welcomed (informed); and made to feel like they are part of something bigger (inspired and engaged). Your organization may be small (or, maybe it's not!); the cause it represents is large.

Donor engagement is a sophisticated phrase for what should be called relationship building. All marketing and communications are for donor engagement and relationship building. No matter how large or small your nonprofit's staff or board is, every individual, every outreach activity and type of communication serves as a potential opportunity for relationship building.

An intentionally designed process for expressing gratefulness in a meaningful way will enhance those relationships. Design it, build it into your day-to-day activity, and gratitude will become an irreplaceable part of your culture.

Build trusting relationships. Connect your cause and your mission with your audience through design touch points, words, and experiences. Trust, engagement, and donations will follow.

KEY INSIGHTS

Be grateful, and acknowledge that the gift is as meaningful to your cause as it is to the donor. Focus on the donor experience to make the process as conversational and meaningful as possible. Keep it simple, and provide assurance that the transaction is safe and secure. Express gratitude for the contribution on screen, via email, and through a personal thank-you note in the mail. The true gift that is given is the supporter's trust. Money, services, or time is an accompaniment to that gift.

Be Trustworthy.

We will seek accountability and transparency, acting and speaking in a manner consistent with our values, character, and culture.

There isn't one particular activity any meaningful cause or organization can do to build trust. Trust is earned over time, on many levels—and it is nurtured whenever there is any kind of interaction between your cause and your audience.

The trust building cycle is simple, and it looks like this. The purpose, character, and culture of your organization are critical connectors between the cause and your audience in the cycle.

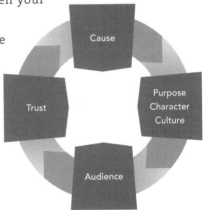

LEADERSHIP BUILDS TRUST

Transparency is often cited as a factor in building trust. Declaring transparency as an operating practice or value makes for good accountability, because as soon as your character or culture shifts away from it, your audience will hold you accountable.

If you declare a *culture* of transparency (in one voice), but act in a manner that is not transparent, the perceived *character* of your organization is that you are not transparent. What you have said does not match up with how you behave.

We have all experienced claims of transparency that were found to be difficult to maintain—not only from a practical perspective, but also from a perceptual perspective. An organization cannot claim to be transparent and accountable, then act in a manner that is contrary to that assertion.

Trust is earned when the audience experiences alignment between the culture, character, and voice of the organization. The trust relationship between the nonprofit that speaks for the cause and the donor or advocate is strengthened. This relationship has to be watched and maintained daily.

CLARITY BUILDS TRUST

Remember: *You can't read the label if you're on the inside of the bottle.* It's not an original insight. It's a good reminder that much of the way in which a cause is valued, and an organization is perceived, is entirely under the control of the audience.

No matter how often an organization creates a communications plan, refines its messaging, or tells stories to advance its mission, there are outside influences that either affirm the character of the organization or tell a different story.

Miscommunication can lead to diminished trust in the organization and the cause it represents. A decrease in funds raised and less volunteer involvement could certainly be a side effect of poor communications.

> 🐦 We will be accountable and transparent, in a manner consistent with our values, character, and culture. #beTrustworthy #causemanifesto

Clarity—the principle of clear and focused communication—can only be achieved when an organization makes its communications choices from the perspective of mission-driven design. Its purpose, culture, character, and voice must be unified in support of the cause.

What's on the Label Should Reflect What's in the Bottle

Donors are increasingly taking a very close look at the organizations they support, starting from the personal/relational (who they know that's involved), and moving to the impersonal/objective (independent reviews). An engagement or public affairs professional needs to be aware that donors view the organization from many different perspectives. A well-considered and executed communications plan will create coherence and continuity for all audiences.

The label on your bottle—your web site, printed collateral, images, and the words that are used—creates the perception you desire. Each touch point should be current, relevant, and truthful.

The Board of Directors Are the Primary Ambassadors

Everybody on a board of directors should be a believer in the cause, demonstrating that belief through active involvement and financial commitment. Donors will ask if the board is 100% committed and if there is 100% support.

- Does your board of directors thoroughly understand the mission, and can they articulate it?
- Are they inspired, and do they wholly support the executive leadership through governance, oversight, and funding?
- Are they engaged, and is this evident in their ambassadorship of the organization?

The Executive Leadership Must Be Available and Approachable

- Every organization needs a "face," a leader that represents not only the organization, but who becomes the voice of the cause. Because of this—whether it's the executive director, president, or board chair—one person will become closely associated with the cause over time.
- The most visible and public leader establishes credibility for donors, becoming a trusted representative of the cause—one to whom a donor will pledge their loyalty through time and giving.

Volunteer Experiences Will Reflect the Culture, the Quality of Communications, and the Value Placed on Their Service

Volunteers not only perceive an organization from an outside perspective; but, because of the nature of what they do, they also often form perceptions based on their volunteer experience. It's critical that the external behavior and character of an organization reflect a volunteer's internal experience.

- Volunteers help advance the cause, and are part of the narrative of the organization. They are ambassadors for the cause, and contributors to the mission.
- How the organization communicates with volunteers indicates the level of respect it has for individuals who donate their time.
- A volunteer's activities are as much about the cause as they are about how serving makes the volunteer feel.
- A volunteer believes their contribution is meaningful and adds value to their life.

Each interaction an advocate, volunteer, donor, or community member has with the organization will create a first or ongoing perception. There must be continuity of voice and experience—from the board, executive leadership, and staff to all communications and volunteer interaction. The message, articulated through stories that inform and inspire, must be clear and compelling, creating credibility and the desire to believe in and love the organization. This process has one objective: to build trust.

KEY INSIGHTS

One thing will never change: *Trust must be earned.* It cannot be bought or created. Nurture a *culture* of trust, and character will follow. Declare a culture of transparency —in one voice—and act in a manner that is consistent with that declaration.

Be Positive.

We will choose our words well, for they will motivate people to follow, donate, advocate, and believe in our cause.

Listening to the vice president of an economic development nonprofit, I heard the comment: "We're a nonprofit. We're boring."

That perspective isn't very inspiring, is it?

From his perspective inside the organization, the mission seemed boring. From outside, the perception could be that their activities are helping regional companies grow their businesses, expand their markets, and create new jobs. Their purpose is helping the private sector to create jobs and make the region stronger as a whole.

I don't see that as boring. A nonprofit doesn't have to be boring. The perspective of purpose and mission is a choice, and the perspective has to be positive.

Boring is when a person tells you the same story they told you the last time you met. Boring is activity that doesn't engage the interest of the participant. Boring is a story that doesn't combine both information and inspiration into a positive message of change and transformation.

Who likes hanging around with a person who is boring, cynical, negative, or a pessimist? By now you've started thinking about the personality of your organization—the attributes that capture its purpose, culture, and character. Is the tone of voice of your communications positive?

Remember when we discussed the organization's voice:

- What is your organization's voice?
- Does your organization speak effectively for the cause?
- Do your communications, activities, and interactions express the culture and character?
- Do all communications consistently speak with one voice?
- What is the tone of the communications?

Words are powerful. Images are powerful. Words and images combined with beautiful typography are even more powerful. When design enhances the stories the narrative is powerful, it inspires hope, and it challenges the listener to action.

> When design conveys hope it challenges the listener to action.

The tone and language that a nonprofit uses to express itself on behalf of the cause are as much a part of design as are the images and typography.

I've listened to how many nonprofits share their stories, communicate their mission, and tell their story to their audiences. Those who speak with one voice, with carefully chosen visual and verbal language, create positive perceptions.

POSITIVE PERCEPTIONS

Over the last 30 years, I've observed the way an organization communicates is a reflection of its internal culture and values. At all levels, character and culture attributes are expressed through behaviors and language, and experienced through design and communications touch points.

This is consistently true for all types of entities: philanthropies, associations, social services, higher education, economic development, environmental—even churches.

Being positive is about more than design and communications. Being positive greatly impacts the goal of engagement, directly impacts the experience one has with an organization, and ultimately impacts an individual's perception of the cause.

Think about a cause you support. How would you describe its voice, its style of expression, and the tone of its communications? Consider this list of adjectives:

- Dynamic
- Encouraging
- Optimistic
- Visionary
- Focused

Which of us wouldn't want to support a cause with those qualities?

But what if the list is slightly different:

- Driven
- Demanding
- Critical
- Single-minded
- Ambiguous

These attributes can leave either positive or negative impressions, in particular when it comes to being positive.

Staff, volunteers, donors, and advocates want an experience that is positive for them. Being positive means bringing fulfillment and meaning to these individuals as they participate in the cause.

Optimism is a better motivator than pessimism. Internally and externally, stakeholders will respond to positive messages with a positive response. A positive experience leads to deeper motivation and more engagement.

Being positive affects everyone's perceptions. Volunteer experiences and donor expectations are directly impacted by the positive and welcoming tone of all design and communications.

After all, the role of good design is *to understand and communicate what your audience is listening for,* not what you think they need to hear.

WHAT IS A POSITIVE EXPERIENCE LIKE?

After many years of serving and observing, it's clear there are four areas where organizations frustrate their volunteers.

Communications: Poor communications is at the core of many frustrations. It may seem basic, but if you clearly communicate who, what, when, where, and why to everybody involved—including the volunteers, audience, organizers, and casual observers—everybody will be on the same page. If you leave any questions unanswered, then response will be negative. If you're not clear, or omit critical information, you will frustrate them.

Expectations: What's *my* role? What's *your* role? Who's

> We will choose our words well, for they will motivate people to follow, donate, advocate, and believe in our cause. **#bePositive #causemanifesto**

in charge? What are my responsibilities? Who's on the team? What are the expectations of those participating in the event in which I'm volunteering? What will I be doing today? Don't be ambiguous with any of these details. Volunteers need to know what is expected of them, so they can serve with their gifts and be effective.

Organization: A volunteer's time is valuable, so don't waste it. You'll find each individual has a specific set of gifts or talents and an interest in serving, so please be prepared when they show up to serve. Don't make them wait while you prepare your presentation, organize materials, or simply get your act together.

Gift making: Donors want to know their gift has meaning and makes an impact. Tell them how, make it possible for them to share, and don't make them guess what the impact is.

It's important not to frustrate volunteers or supporters. They want to serve with their gifts, not get frustrated. They want to be motivated, not demotivated. They want to *serve* with joy, and *receive* meaning from their service. It's one responsibility of leadership to help make that happen.

A bit of behavioral psychology and profiling may be in order, to understand what motivates (and demotivates) key volunteer leaders. Short of that, making expectations of their roles clear, and then equipping and *empowering* individuals to serve, can make up for behavior analysis. If an individual is capable of leading, empower and support them in that leadership role.

Share your performance expectations, and give volunteer leaders the authority to execute their responsibilities and the communication resources they need to succeed. Effective communications will improve everybody's experience.

Organizational communication isn't always clear—even with web sites, texts, email, and phones. As a business professional, I would never consider conducting business with clients by text, yet it seems to be an acceptable way to conduct relationships with volunteer leaders. Leadership by texting is highly ineffective.

Nonprofit leaders can't be completely aware of what's happening at the volunteer level unless they are in continuous dialog with observers and participants in volunteering. Too often, valid observations from volunteers are perceived as complaints; suggestions that a business organization would consider for continuous improvement are perceived as annoyances. There is little room for true innovation, because the "best practices" of other organizations—that may or may not be applicable to your organization's particular circumstances—are used as the model for innovation and change.

Focus on the relationships and management will be easier. Relationships are what create loyal followers and affinity for the cause. Create fewer distractions and provide more focus. Volunteers show up to serve; it's your responsibility to make certain they are equipped and have a positive experience.

CREATING POSITIVE COMMUNICATIONS
AND A POSITIVE CULTURE

It's not as difficult as you might think to be positive with your words. Start with your outcomes, your successes, and positive impact, and work backwards from there.

List five areas in which you're having a positive impact:
1.
2.
3.
4.
5.

List five successes your nonprofit has experienced in the last 12 months:
1.
2.
3.
4.
5.

List five positive outcomes from your programs within the last 12 months:
1.
2.
3.
4.
5.

List five positive words you can use in your communication planning that will help you convey the positive impact and perceptions that you want your audience to share:

1.

2.

3.

4.

5.

EXPERIENCE NEEDS TO BE POSITIVE

Any nonprofit must balance its desire to achieve its mission and fulfill the cause with two objectives. First, every organization needs to ensure its volunteers have a superb volunteer experience. Second, donors need to feel as if their gifts and contributions are valued and acknowledged. The cause and your mission will move forward more effectively when volunteers and donors feel appreciated. Think of them as participants and partners—respect their time and value their contributions. If you don't, they will find an organization that does appreciate them.

Does your organization have a designated donor relations and volunteer relations coordinator? Should it? Of course, it depends on the size of your organization, the number of volunteers it works with, and the relationship it has with its donors.

If you think your volunteer's experience can be more positive, a great way to start is by saying *thank you*. It's all part of cultivating and stewarding the most important external supporters you have.

KEY INSIGHTS

Optimism is a better motivator than pessimism. Internally and externally, stakeholders will respond to positive messages with a positive response. A positive experience leads to deeper motivation and more engagement. Being positive affects everyone's perceptions. Volunteer experiences and donor expectations are directly impacted by the positive and welcoming tone of all design and communications.

Be Powerful.

We will believe our cause is meaningful, and act in the belief that it has the power to change the world.

Power comes from within. A powerful cause is one that you believe will be transformational, as it works to fulfill its purpose and achieve its mission. You have to believe it will create change in people's lives and circumstances. You have to believe others will find meaning in the cause, and reach out to those individuals.

Power is not timid, it is not tentative—yet neither is it arrogant. The most effective, powerful leaders are servant leaders—those who demonstrate their belief in their cause through their actions and with their voice.

Power comes from strength: a courageous and engaged board; a confident and competent leader; a clearly articulated purpose; and a mission embodied by the character, culture, and voice of the organization.

Powerful causes embody leadership, not only internally, but also in the nonprofit community. I can think of several nonprofit entities that are looked upon by the grantmaking and philanthropic community as leaders in the nonprofit community. These groups show, through their actions, a willingness to collaborate, and are an example within their spheres of influence.

Not every organization will be as powerful as these. Not every individual will personally identify with your purpose and mission.

You can never stop believing and acting in the belief that your cause has the power to change the world. If *you* don't believe, then who will?

WE'VE ALWAYS DONE IT THAT WAY

Design and communication are integral to projecting a powerful image; I would consider them essential.

Many nonprofits think the "B" word is the way to make their organization appear powerful. Boards of directors consider a new web site as a tool for "strengthening their brand." Perhaps the marketing or development committee suggests a "re-brand" by commissioning a new visual identity, as if a face lift will be sufficient to create a new perception.

Was any research commissioned to learn what perceptions the audience has of the organization? In reality, it would be the stakeholders that apply their perceptions to your organization. This may simply be an attempt to control the aspects of what you consider a brand: the logo and the marketing communications that the logo is applied to.

Branding, in its original context, refers to the searing of a mark on the hide of a horse in order to identify it as belonging to a specific owner. Ranchers brand cattle in order to make it easier to sort them out if they get mixed in with another herd. Understandably, this process is painful for the horse or cow.

The rancher controls the branding process, searing every animal with the same mark, in the same way. As it "heals up and hairs over," its appearance changes; the mark itself may become invisible to the viewer, as if nothing was ever done at all.

WHAT'S REALLY HAPPENING

"Sacred cows make great steak dinners."

This quote is a popular concept about how to shift thinking and consider problems, circumstances, and challenges in a new way. In other words, challenging the status quo.

Sacred cows are those processes and practices that never change. They represent the status quo, the same way of doing things that seems to have worked before. It even has a name: *Founder's Syndrome*. For an entity within the tax-exempt, philanthropic, or higher education sector, it's evident when founders or boards of directors don't adapt their management, governance, or oversight methods as their organization grows or changes.

If you think your organization is currently experiencing symptoms of Founder's Syndrome, a quick Internet search will tell you everything you need to know about it and may help to confirm your diagnosis.

> Without a strategic plan to guide a communication plan, and without leadership that understands the role of mission-driven design, it's common to see the same principles and practices from the private sector applied to the nonprofit sector—whether they work or not.

Without a strategic plan to guide a communication plan, and without leadership that understands the role of mission-driven design, it's common to see the same principles and practices from the private sector applied to the nonprofit sector—whether they work or not. Sometimes this approach strengthens the organization and it becomes more powerful, but in other instances this approach weakens it.

Fortunately, Founder's Syndrome is curable—it just takes courage.

THE CAUSE IS MORE POWERFUL THAN A BRAND

Your organization is not a horse—or a brand. In the mind of the potential volunteer, advocate, or donor, it's not the visual identity that distinguishes your nonprofit from the next. Your brand is not what makes your organization powerful.

Your cause is not a brand. Your organization is not a brand; it has an identity—a purpose, character, and culture that you help to create—and it becomes powerful by speaking with one voice on behalf of the cause.

The reality is that, with regard to the perception of your organization, you are not in control. What everybody else perceives about your organization is what's important. It's not what you think about your cause, it's what *they* think.

Many of the sacred cows engaged in by nonprofits involve design and communications. Committees are set up for branding, marketing, development, and outreach without addressing the real need. Some valid considerations include: Is the organization focused? Does it have a strategic plan? Do the culture, character, and values that guide the organization's mission align with the values of their audience?

Many nonprofits begin and end their talk about branding with the visual aspects of identity. When nonprofit

> 🐦 We will believe our cause is meaningful, and act in the belief that it has the power to change the world. #bePowerful #causemanifesto

institutions or organizations are struggling, it's easy to consider that a face lift will solve the problems, and give the appearance that the issues have been addressed.

Visual identity is just one part of the engagement continuum, and the board must be aware of how all aspects of nonprofit communications affect this continuum, in order to fund and empower the executive director and staff to advance the cause.

We live in a world of perceptions. Everything we see, hear, and experience creates a perception in our minds of the cause or organization with which we are interacting. To the stakeholder, perception is reality; what they think about the cause or organization is more real to them than what you've told them.

IT'S NOT ABOUT BRAND, IT'S ABOUT IDENTITY AND PERCEPTIONS

A colleague, an attorney with a county prosecutor's office, explained how he used his choice of tie to create a perception in the courtroom. On days he was introducing himself to a jury, he chose a pale blue tie for its calming affect. For days he would be cross-examining a witness, he would choose a red tie, a color of power and authority. Each color was chosen to create a specific perception.

Look around the boardroom, and you'll experience how your colleagues project an image of themselves based simply on what they are wearing. As you interact around the board table, you'll hear how they talk; you may also interact with them in a business or social setting. You'll see how they act, and gain insight into their character through their behavior (their personal culture). All of these senses and interactions combine to create your impression of each individual and, collectively, the whole of the board. The external and internal create a complete identity (in your mind) of that individual. Their appearance, their words, and their actions show you their character and sense of culture.

This analogy applies to the nonprofit that the board governs (whether a cause-specific organization or philanthropy). Each touch point of donor, advocate, and volunteer experience is a critical point of interaction that attracts, informs, inspires, engages, and stewards the relationship between the individual and their values and the organization and its values.

We identify with causes and organizations we like. We can't help but to form a perception based on the way something, or somebody, appears to our eyes. Even if, to all outward appearances, that perception is one of power and strength, only time will tell if it is backed up by words and actions.

BEYOND ATTRACTION

Some organizations focus purely on the attraction phase of the Engagement Continuum, which creates an unstable and unsustainable culture. In this culture, staff and the board are constantly reacting to priorities of the moment, and the tyranny of the urgent. Planning is an afterthought; getting by from week to week is the most important consideration. Little attention is paid to stewarding supporter relationships or executing a strategic plan developed jointly by the board and executive management.

This is evident when tactical marketing and events are substituted for sustainable and strategic communications outreach. Event-driven outreach creates a culture in which staff is reacting to event deadlines, instead of steadily executing outreach initiatives that were identified by the strategic planning process.

Attraction is only the first step on the engagement continuum, with the ultimate goal being stewardship and advancement—the individual assuming the role of an ambassador for the cause.

When the goal of attraction is to create a body of ambassadors, attraction's role will be properly understood and implemented. The steps of the engagement continuum that are in between cannot be overlooked.

Attraction is effective at introducing people to an organization but never at informing and inspiring people about a cause. If your goal is to only make an introduction, there will be a continual need to attract. Until a strategy is in place to inform and inspire individuals along the engagement continuum, there will be little motivation for supporters who want to be engaged to maintain interest in the organization. Nurturing affinity for the cause will create engagement with the organization. Your supporters will be ambassadors and advocates, enthusiastically supporting the cause.

AS MUCH AS IT'S NOT ABOUT THE STORY, IT'S ABOUT THE FOUNDATION OF THE STORY

Powerful stories have three elements: pathos (emotion), logos (rationality), and ethos (credibility). Emotion and rationality, woven into the narrative, builds credibility.

- Pathos literally means "from the heart," and deals with emotion. It builds an emotional connection with the audience, through story. Emotions are motivators. (This is how a story inspires.)
- Logos is a logical argument, based on statistics, facts, and evidence. The facts speak to our mind. (This is how a story informs.)
- Ethos is the combination of pathos and logos that builds credibility (or the character) of the speaker.

Engagement creates community, as individuals become part of the narrative (the story) that nonprofits tell. Good stories draw the reader in and make them feel like they are part of the action. A good nonprofit story will create a connection between the listener and the storyteller; if the story involves a way that the listener can participate, then engagement occurs.

Think of a story such as *Lord of the Rings*. While it is a story of good vs. evil and the journey to overcome that evil, there is also a love story woven throughout the narrative that transcends the conflict and its resolution.

Can you create a love story from the perspective of mission-driven design? It might be worth trying. Inspire your audience by appealing to them from your heart to their heart. Tell them why yours is a meaningful cause with facts and information that speak to their mind. To build your credibility, use your unique identity and voice consistently and authentically, to project a powerful image of the impact your organization is making.

What is there to love about your cause, and how can you tell that story in a powerful way to inspire your followers?

KEY INSIGHTS

To earn trust, tell a powerful story that speaks to the mind but appeals to the heart. As the stories are told in a manner that is consistent with your character and culture, they will connect the mission with the audience. To be powerful is to be a leader, and to influence your followers and your peers.

Be Courageous.

We will dream big dreams,
and have the courage
to change and adapt
in order to make
our vision a reality.

Perhaps you're thinking: *"How is courage relevant to mission-driven design and raising your voice above the noise?"*

Are you a leader? Leaders need to be courageous. Most likely, you're operating within your comfort zone, fulfilling a specific role within your organization and within your community. Perhaps you're hesitant to try, or even suggest, a new way of connecting with your audience; reluctant to challenge your board to increase funding for design and communications; or afraid to admit that you just don't know where to begin.

You do want to change the world, don't you? Make a difference? Have impact?

Then you need to share that with the world. Boldly. Courageously. Confidently.

You need to have an oversized belief in your purpose. You need to believe that what you are on a mission to do is the most important thing in the world.

Those who have small dreams only look to the path ahead and think about what tomorrow brings. Those who dream big

> 🐦 Dream big dreams. Have the courage to adapt and change in order to make those dreams a reality. **#beCourageous #causemanifesto**

dreams see beyond the horizon and plan for a future reality. Colin Powell has said, "Leaders inspire people to reach beyond themselves."

Courage may require that you step into the unknown. It may require difficult conversations. It will require that you find a way to overcome whatever fear is preventing you from taking the next step.

Do you understand that your work is not about you or your organization? It's about the success of your stakeholders—their stories and their impact on education, entrepreneurship, economic development, health and wellness, sustainability, philanthropy, the arts, and other meaningful causes?

Are you confident that your work has a significant impact on the initiatives and programs on which you've collaborated? Are you grateful for the opportunities to be a resource to the remarkable and increasingly interconnected organizations with which you collaborate?

It takes courage to admit: "It's not about us; it's about the cause and those we serve."

"Ah" you say, "our funders and audience will think spending money on design and communications is wasteful and doesn't contribute to the delivery of programs and services." That's nonsense. If they do think that, then it's time to re-educate them. How can you expect to have impact if you're unable to raise new funds and create more awareness in order to attract and engage more donors? Be courageous!

It takes courage to ask a grantmaking organization to fund design and communications that will enable a nonprofit to reach a wider audience. It takes courage to educate donors on how and why communications is a vital, yet overlooked, aspect of cause communications and program delivery.

It takes courage for a board of directors to rise to the challenge of funding design and communications. It takes courage for the board to rise to the challenge of funding the organization in a sustainable manner.

It's not a matter of *how* to communicate courage, but a matter of communicating *with* courage.

What will it take for *you* to be courageous?

KEY INSIGHTS

Those who dream big dreams see beyond the horizon and plan for a future reality. It takes courage to admit: "It's not about us; it's about the cause and those we serve."

Resources

From the Preface
Nonprofit Answer Guide, a project of Center for Nonprofit Management (nonprofitanswerguide.org)

From Part One: Chapter Four
The organization to which I refer is the Samuel Szabo Foundation (samuelszabofoundation.org)

From Part One: Chapter Five
- Giving USA research (givingusareports.org)
- Hootsuite.com
- Twitonomy.com
- Joomla! (joomla.org)

From Part One: Chapter Six

- *The Communication Toolkit*, from Cause Communications
  http://www.causecommunications.org/download-signup.
  php?id=toolkit
- The web address for the NTEE Classification System
  was shortened; the full address is
  http://nccs.urban.org/classification/NTEE.cfm
- *Leap of Reason*, by Mario Morino (leapofreason.org)

From Part One: Chapter Seven

IDEO's free Human-Centered Design Toolkit
(ideo.com/work/human-centered-design-toolkit/)

From Part Two: Chapter Four

- The web address for Dan Pallotta's TED talk
  was shortened; the full address is
  ted.com/talks/dan_pallotta_the_way_we_think_about_
  charity_is_dead_wrong.html
- Charity Navigator: charitynavigator.org
- GuideStar: guidestar.org
- Better Business Bureau Wise Giving Alliance Standards
  for Charity Accountability: bbb.org/charity-reviews
- Klout: klout.com

All trademarks referenced in this book are the property of their respective companies.

For additional resources, visit causemanifesto.org

Acknowledgments

I have learned that books do not flow forth from the writer's fingers like a spring, but grow like a bonsai tree. This book was a slow sculpture, carefully and diligently tended, trimmed, and pruned. The writing, design, and editing took 18 months; the preparation took 30 years.

I'm very grateful to my wife and business partner, Lisa Sooy, for her unwavering support. Thank you for the freedom to write on so many Saturday mornings. Thank you for trusting me, and taking the risk with me to launch Aespire. I could not do this without you.

I appreciate the opportunity to work with leaders, board members, volunteers, and colleagues within the nonprofit community, both personally and professionally. Your passion and dedication to the causes you believe in are boundless. You are making a difference.

I would not have considered writing this book, had it not been for the suggestion of David C. Baker. I trust I have risen to the challenge you set forth, and this is a book of which you and the RockBench authors can be proud. I do not know what prompted you to challenge me to write it. This book is proof that the work you do matters.

Thank you to Blair Enns for the coaching and encouragement, as we both realized that expertise plus perspective creates credibility. In my persistence, I have become a smarter student. You're an excellent teacher.

I appreciate the creativity, endless patience, and exquisite attention to detail provided by designer Vance Williams. Thank you for putting my commas in the correct places.

Thank you to Matt Dray, Robert Slatt, and Vance Williams for your dedication to Aespire and the causes we serve.

Thank you to Julie Chase-Morefield, Denver Daniel, Scott Humphreys, Patty O'Brien, and so many others for your feedback and insights on this work. Thank you to the reviewers, who gave freely of their time and shared their honest assessments of my work.

Thank you to Brian Frederick, Frank Whitfield, and those who helped refine the principles of the Cause Manifesto.

Thank you to Bev for reading my blog and telling me how the Manifesto made a difference to you.

And last, but not least, this book would not have been written without vast amounts of hazelnut coffee.

Be Grateful.

Colophon

Cover and Interior Design
Vance Williams, Aespire®
Designed with Adobe InDesign CC and Adobe Illustrator CC

Typefaces for the Type Lovers
- Titling typeface: Avenir, designed by Adrian Frutiger, 1988 for LinoType GmbH
- Body typeface: PMN Caecilia, designed by Peter Matthias Noordzij, 1983 for LinoType GmbH

Proofreading and Editing
Vance Williams and Donna McGuire

The author's last name is pronounced *soy*, as in *soy bean* or *soy sauce*. All other similarities end there.